MW01248508

R.U.N.
FOR LIFE

DAVE ANSELL

R.U.N for LIFE
Copyright © 2009
by Dave Ansell

Unless otherwise noted, all Scripture quotations are from the Holy Bible, New International Version. Copyright © 1973, 1978, 1984, International Bible Society. Used by Permission.

Scripture quotations marked:
CEV—from the Holy Bible, Contemporary English Version. Copyright © 1995, American Bible Society. Used by permission.
KJV—from the Holy Bible, King James Version.
NKJV—from the Holy Bible, New Century Version. Copyright © 2005. Thomas Nelson, Inc. Used by permission.
NKJV—from the Holy Bible, New King James Version. Copyright © 1982 by Thomas Nelson, Inc. Used by permission.
NLT—from the Holy Bible, New Living Translation. Copyright © 1996, Tyndale House Publishers. Used by permission.
NLV—from the Holy Bible, New Life Version. Copyright © 1969 by Christian Literature International. Used by permission.
TM—from The Message, © 1993, 2000, 2002 by Eugene H. Peterson. Used by permission.

All rights reserved. No part of this publication may be reproduced, stored in a retrieval system, or transmitted in any form by means electronic, mechanical, photocopying, recording or otherwise, except for the inclusion of brief quotations in a review, without prior permission in writing from the publisher. The use of short quotations or occasional page copying for personal or group study is permitted and encouraged.

ISBN: 978-0-9817608-2-7

Published by

LIFEBRIDGE
B O O K S
P.O. BOX 49428
CHARLOTTE, NC 28277

Printed in the United States of America.

DEDICATION

*This book is dedicated to all of the dreamers
in this world who dare to believe that God uses
ordinary people for extraordinary causes. To people
like the Hovis family who have experienced life
alterations and have chosen to Never Give Up!
You inspire us all to R.U.N for LIFE!*

"I have had the wonderful privilege of doing ministry with Dave Ansell for nearly ten years. It is obvious to me that Dave has fallen in love with the Body of Christ. His passionate love for the church compels him to communicate the Gospel in a way that draws seekers to the Cross, while challenging believers to go deeper with God."

– Luke Barnett, Executive Pastor,
Phoenix First Assembly

CONTENTS

ONE

AWAKENING
THE DREAM

*Do you not know that in a race all
the runners run, but only one gets the
prize? Run in such a way as to get the prize.
Everyone who competes in the games goes into
strict training. They do it to get a crown that
will not last; but we do it to get a
crown that will last forever.*
– 1 CORINTHIANS 9:24-27

The curtain has come down and the torch has been dramatically extinguished in Beijing, China, but the dreams of the athletes that made it to the podium in the 2008 Olympics will live on for years to come.

We will always remember the look of pride on swimmer Michael Phelps' face as he made his way to his mother Debbie to celebrate his record breaking eighth gold medal to surpass Mark Spitz. We witnessed Jamaica's Usain Bolt indisputably become the world's fastest man, and it's highly probable that the smiling girl from Des Moines, Iowa, Shawn Johnson, will grace the front of a Wheaties® box for her achievement of finally winning her gold medal.

While these three athletes may stand out from many other world class Olympians, there is something all of them have in common. They all possess a dream.

Athletes train for years for this one moment in time to have a chance to win the gold medal. It's the dream of being a gold medal winner that motivates an athlete to get up in the early hours of the morning and start rigorous training. They understand that today's self-discipline ultimately decides who will stand in the winning spotlight, as their country's flag is raised high.

THE SECRET OF GREATNESS

"I have a dream!" The words from the speech of Martin Luther King, Jr., continue to inspire millions around the world.

There is power in a dream:

- It can lift a heart out of despair.
- It can put joy back into a life.
- It will challenge the mediocrity that tries to seep into our soul.
- It will motivate us to wake up in the morning and live.

- It can rekindle our relationship with the Giver of dreams, Jesus Christ.
- It will cause you to lean into the strength of God.
- It will inspire you to dream lofty dreams that in your own strength seem impossible to accomplish.

A dream becomes truly great when you understand that you need God involved to make it a reality.

No dream is exceptional until the Author of dreams is invited to participate in the process. And it is my prayer that each reader will allow Him to renew life in their heart today.

--------▲--------

May something happen that is so energizing, so transformational, it will change the direction of your journey in the here and now and set you on a course that will take your breath away.

Together, may we learn what it means to RUN for LIFE.

"YOU'RE BREATHTAKING!"

I believe there is enough evidence to conclude that a God-given dream exists in the heart of every individual. I am convinced that the Almighty implanted a custom dream in your soul before the world ever laid eyes on you. *"Oh yes, you shaped me first inside, then out; you formed me in my mother's womb. I thank you, High God—You're breathtaking! Body and soul, I am marvelously made! I worship in adoration—what a creation! You know me inside and out, You know every bone in my body; You know exactly how I was made, bit-by-bit, how I was sculpted from nothing into something. Like an open book, You watched me grow from conception to birth; all the stages of my life were spread out before you, The days of my life all prepared before I'd even lived one day"* (Psalm 139:13 TM).

————▲————

We serve an awesome, mighty, dream-giving God!

In every champion you've ever heard about you will undoubtedly find the evidence of a childhood dream. The problem for many of us is that the vision has been suffocated by the disappointments of life—which leaves us living below our redemptive potential. A few hard knocks, and we start lowering the expectation levels of our life until finally the dream can no longer be visualized. We stop believing that God wants to accomplish something marvelous through us.

THE DOUBTERS

Even the smartest and most famous dreamers have expressed doubts concerning their dreams, and other's dreams as well. Albert Einstein remarked in 1932: *"There is not the slightest indication that nuclear energy will ever be obtainable."*

Thomas Edison thought alternating current would be a waste of time.

Franklin Delano Roosevelt once predicted (when he was the Assistant Secretary of the Navy): *"Airplanes would never be useful in battle against a fleet of ships."*

In 1883, Lord Kelvin, president of the Royal Society of Scotland, predicted: *"X-rays will prove to be a hoax."*

"Everything that can be invented has been invented." This was announced by Charles H. Duell, commissioner of the U.S. Patents Office, in 1899.

There is nothing like the passage of time to prove the world's geniuses wrong!

A noted motivational speaker hands out multicolored pencils to his audience as he makes the following declaration: *"You are the author of your own destiny, your own dreams, history is waiting to be written by you."*

While I respect the national attention that he is getting and I commend his contribution to awakening the expectations of hearts and lives, I would challenge his statement with a contrary thought; namely, that history has already been written—and all one has to do is excavate what God has already laid in the heart of man.

Your heavenly Father has placed a dream in your heart. He is its Author and Finisher. So you don't have to conjure up a dream or write it as the sole author:

11

God wants to reveal to you what He already has planned for your future.

CONNECT WITH THE CREATOR

I believe the Almighty desires to partner with each of us to unearth his or her dream. Rather than handing out multi-colored pencils, we should be passing out excavating tools. It would be a little bulky to take home and not very cost effective, but it would be more appropriate to offer shovels, picks, and brushes—symbols that God is doing a work in our lives.

We simply need to connect with the Creator, the Author of the vision, and have attentive ears as He coaches us toward Gold Medal living.

————▲————

There's a purpose waiting to spring alive in your heart. Now is the time to awaken the seed the Lord has planted within you.

God loves dreamers. In Hebrews chapter 11 there is a major list of such special people:

- Jacob had a dream of receiving the blessings of his father Isaac.
- Joseph had a God-given dream of preserving a nation.
- Moses had a vision of leading the Israelites out of captivity.

- Joshua had a dream to take the baton of leadership from Moses. The Lord said, "Just follow Me and lead the children of Israel into the Promised Land."
- Rahab, a prostitute, had a dream of being found in the favor of the Lord and she is listed in God's Hall of Fame—proof that our potential is not limited by our past when the Father is connected to our future.

The Bible is filled with men and women who were divinely inspired:

- David dreamed of being a king.
- Esther had a vision of standing up for God's people. She understood that she was created for this moment in time to be used of the Lord to save His people from destruction.
- Samuel dreamed of being the one who would find the next ruler of Israel.

Each responded to a nudge to step out of their comfort zone and pursue their dream.

DON'T GET TRAPPED

But what exactly is a God-given dream? First and foremost, it is FORWARD LOOKING. It is thinking of where God wants to take you in spite of where you are today. There are far too many people trapped in the present.

I was attending a conference at a hotel in Anaheim, California, with a couple thousand Christian leaders. When you gather that many people into one hotel, the elevators can be extremely slow as they stop at every floor. The need for exercise and having chronic impatience gave me the motivation I needed to use the stairwells to get around the hotel. It was brilliant!

Seated in the large conference room I imagined all these attendees waiting in a crammed elevator like a bunch of experimental mice. I thought, "These people need to start thinking outside the box."

Leaving the auditorium toward the end of one of the meetings and wanting to beat the crowd, I slipped out trying to avoid being noticed. (I think it was my way of getting back at those who leave church services early!)

As I made my grand escape, I took an immediate left and saw signs from heaven. Ten doors that had the letters *"E-X-I-T"* in bold red were God's provision for escapees! When I pushed open one of the doors and bolted down the stairwell, suddenly I realized, this was an emergency exit. Feeling like a fool, I thought, *"No big deal, I'll just run back up and slip out of the door and pretend that I was investigating the safety of the hotel."*

Getting back to the top of the stairs and noticing there were no inside handles to open the doors left me trapped in my embarrassment. It was one of those Southwest Airlines moments, *"Want to get away?"*

I was now the one pacing around like a mouse in a maze. Frustrated, I thought, "I must find a way to avoid a couple thousand people thinking, *'What an idiot!'*"

"In Case of Emergency"

While trying to figure out how to get out of this predicament it was clear that other victims had been trapped in this twilight zone.

It was of little comfort to learn I was not the first to walk into this trap. Near the doors that were conspicuously missing handles, the walls were defaced with handwritten notes from previous captives. Words I would never say almost seemed appropriate. To my shame, I found myself nodding in agreement and desiring a pen to support the angst of my fellow prisoners.

After several minutes of calculating my options, it was now time to make my move. I could bang on the doors with a holy terror or find a way to pry open the door. It was part humiliation and part revenge that led me to pull a metal sign off the wall that read, "In case of emergency break glass."

This was no credible emergency, so I just ripped the sign off the wall and left the adjacent glass intact. Then, carefully, I slipped the metal plate down the crack in the doorframe and slid open the lock. Whew!

Within minutes I was standing among civilization

again hoping no one noticed the sweat pouring down my face. (By the way, I left the metal sign leaning against one of the doors for the next victim!)

God Requires the Impossible

The truth is, we all get in positions where we would rather not admit that we made a blunder. Our dreams get trapped inside without any visible way of being released from captivity.

If your dreams seem imprisoned today, don't lose heart. God can provide a way of escape. He is the great Dream Releaser.

In fact, God requires impossible situations as a prerequisite to partnership. He refuses to partner with limited dreams that can be accomplished without His assistance. Those kind of dreams leave people with big heads and small hearts.

Today is the day to dream—but whatever you dream—dream BIG! Your invitation to God will lead you to dream bigger than ever, so get ready for the ride of your life!

Who is Carrying You?

I am reminded of the story of an elephant and a mouse. The mouse was anxious to get a free ride over an old wooden suspension bridge so he jumped on the back of an elephant that was heading across. As the elephant took his first few steps and kept walking, the bridge began to sway precariously back and forth and the mouse soon found himself hanging on for dear life!

When they reached the other side and the mouse looked back at the swaying bridge, he leaned towards the ear of the elephant and exclaimed, "We really shook that thing didn't we?"

This is exactly our mistaken view on life sometimes. We think we are the ones making this huge impact, while in reality we are being safely carried by God Almighty.

"EXPAND MY FAITH"

Where should we begin?

Let me challenge you to do something specific. Although this may seem awkward, I am asking you to stop right now and ask God to rekindle the dream that is latent in your heart.

————▲————

Things may seem unclear and your future may be clouded, but begin to ask the Author to reveal His plan and purpose for your life.

So go ahead—put the book down and pray a simple prayer: *"God awaken the dream in me, Lord do what only You can do. I pray that You would enlarge my scope and expand my faith. Help me to see with new eyes. God awaken the dream in me. In Jesus name, Amen."*

Friend, if you prayed with sincerity, get ready for God to answer in a mighty way. He is going to challenge you to step out onto the field of faith and chase the dream, because He delights in answering prayers like this.

THEY DIED RUNNING!

A brief look at the accounts in scripture of the dreamers listed in God's Hall of Fame unveils an interesting fact. These great examples of faith didn't have the chance to see all of their dreams come true. It wasn't that which they envisioned never happened; it certainly did. But their dreams were so big they extended beyond their life-span.

These outstanding saints died while they were pursuing God's purposes. They died running! Take a look at Hebrews 11:13: *"All these people were still living by faith when they died. They did not receive the things promised; they only saw them from a distance."*

———— ▲ ————

Never forget that a God-given dream is "Forward-Looking."

18

For example, let's look at Moses. At forty years of age he decided to follow the dream God had placed within him. He discarded all the rewards of an opulent lifestyle. What the Lord showed him exceeded the pursuit of riches. The Bible tells us, *"He chose to be mistreated along with the people of God rather than to enjoy the pleasures of sin for a short time. He regarded disgrace for the sake of Christ as of greater value than the treasures of Egypt, because he was looking ahead to his reward. By faith he left Egypt, not fearing the king's anger; he persevered <u>because he saw him who is invisible</u>"* (Hebrews 11:25-27).

Who did he see? He saw Jesus Christ. Do you understand that Moses was so forward looking that he envisioned the Messiah thousands of years before there was a virgin named Mary? He saw Jesus coming to this earth to redeem mankind. Now that's a vision!

LIVING WITHOUT LIMITS

God's dreams for us are bigger than our finite minds can imagine. So never limit the Creator.

Moses was able to see the Sacrifice before it was ever made known to the world. And it outpaced him by a millennium or more.

Here is a question which is begging to be asked, "Why would anyone pursue a dream that they may never see come to fruition? Why would a person expend time and energy toward an objective they may not have the opportunity to enjoy?"

When we have God's endorsement for a dream, He determines the distance you will run and when it is time to pass the baton. Some visions are so great in scope it takes an entire team of individuals to run the distance.

———————▲———————

Never underestimate the power of what the Lord places inside each of us.

THE GREAT ADVENTURE

A God-given dream is "Forward Looking," but there is another truth worth sharing. A God-given dream is also an ADVENTURE. In other words, there is joy in the process.

I love The Message version on this topic. It says in Proverbs 2:1-5: *"Good friend, take to heart what I'm telling you; collect my counsels and guard them with your life. Tune your ears to the world of Wisdom; set your heart on a life of Understanding. That's right—if you make Insight your priority, and won't take no for an answer, searching for it like a prospector panning for gold, like an adventurer on a treasure hunt, believe me, before you know it Fear-of-God will be yours; you'll have come upon the Knowledge of God."*

What we are talking about here is not a forty-yard dash. It's more like a triathlon. Moses' forty years in the desert would support this point. It's the variety of challenges that come our way which make up a God-given dream.

As a vision is being fulfilled there are countless stories to be told of overcoming great obstacles, conquering insurmountable odds, battling the temptation to quit, and experiencing the exhilaration of crossing the finish line. It's the adventure that makes the dream worth the pursuit.

Every morning when we wake up we should be excited because there is a story being written while we are pursuing God's purpose. Each day there is a potential for a personal "breaking news" story.

OH, THE MIRACLES!

The most noteworthy accounts recorded in the Old and New Testament are from individuals who overcame major obstacles. They were facing impossible odds.

Think about what took place at the Red Sea. Nobody ever envisioned crossing this body of water via dry land. But there was a dream in the heart of Moses to lead the children of Israel out of captivity and the adventure included God saying, *"I'm going to take you through the Red Sea."*

Imagine for a moment the faces etched with expressions of emotional and physical exhaustion as they are running away from Pharaoh's pursuing army. Can you hear them recounting the story after the miraculous crossing? Sitting around, one comments: *"Boy I cannot believe it. I will never forget when God split that sea in two and made a way for us right down the middle!"* Another chimes in: *"You should have seen your face! You were so afraid!"*

Every person had a story to tell. Can you imagine over a million people crossing on dry ground? Then, the moment Pharaoh's army stepped in the Red Sea, there was a another miracle. As the people of Israel stood and watched the armies of Egypt being swallowed up in the waters, they understood that their God was a Deliverer and He does the impossible.

Oh, the stories that were told. They were probably passing out T-shirts emblazoned with, "I survived the Red Sea and all I got was this lousy shirt!"

But remember this. If there hadn't been a dream there would be no Red Sea miracle. It's the adventure that adds the excitement.

----------▲----------

Rejoice when you face insurmountable odds because God is carving out a dream and giving you an amazing story to tell for His glory.

Manna falling from heaven and water springing from a rock? When they later told these stories around the campfire, I'm sure it made those listening sit on the edge of the rock in rapt attention. They could almost see the dust flying off the hooves of those horses as Pharaoh's army started racing down that hill. You

22

could sense the tension. You could visualize Moses grabbing the arm of a slave driver and saying: *"NO MORE! You will not beat this man another time. Let my people go!"*

THE HIDDEN MOMENTS

To my knowledge, nobody envisioned that the walls of Jericho would collapse. It was just part of the story that was being written while the people of Israel pursued their dream—so we also would learn some life-changing lessons and still talk about them today.

The noted pastor, Bill Hybels, believes: *"The most important moments in your life are not the 'big ones'...rather, they are the private moments, the hidden moments when God gives you a leading."*

Catch what the Lord is saying, because He is speaking to us all the time and wants us to obey the "little things." We cannot fathom how large such small concepts or incidents will become. These are the moments that make chasing the dream so fulfilling.

HANG ON!

You may be facing an obstacle right now. The dust may be falling upon you as the reality of a foreclosure, or mounting bills are racing your way. Maybe it's a medical condition and the doctors have told you,

"There is little hope."

During the writing of this book one of our church members was given a grim diagnosis with twenty-four hours to live. We began to pray as a body of believers and soon the doctor changed the immediate timetable and announced, "We're going to take it day to day."

The church continued to be in prayer.

Then one morning, the man awoke and began to communicate, which the doctors thought was impossible. But the physicians cautioned: *"Don't get too carried away because this does not mean he is going to make a recovery."*

Days turned into a week, then two weeks—and, praise God, today he is home and active again in the life of the church.

God still specializes in things thought impossible, so we must never give up.

The famed British prime minister, Winston Churchill, once said: *"The nose of a bulldog is slanted backwards so he can continue to breathe without letting go."*

Hang on! There's a dream that God is awakening in your heart!

"I CAN"

Jesus said to His disciples: *"With man this is impossible, but with God all things are possible"* (Mark 10:27).

So what is your dream? What are you asking God for? Never say, "It can't be done."

The Lord is waiting for someone like you who is daring enough to step into the impossible. Remove the word "can't" from your vocabulary, in faith believe: *"I can do all things through him who gives me strength"* (Philippians 4:13).

Follow the Holy Spirit's guidance because you never know where He's going to lead and what amazing accomplishments He can produce through you.

THE DESIRES OF YOUR HEART

It is also essential to know that your *PASSIONS* fuel a God-given dream.

———▲———

You were uniquely created by the Almighty, and there is a custom-made seed planted within you that is designed to recreate energy in the pursuit of God's purpose.

The Lord knows how to encourage and empower us on our journey. One of the ways He achieves this is by blessing us with the yearnings of our hearts. He knitted those longings within us and loves to show us His favor.

Be encouraged in this promise: *"Delight yourself in*

the Lord and He will give you the desires of your heart" (Psalm 37:4).

DIVINE REJUVENATION

Abraham had a vision to move from living in tents to establish a city: *"For he was looking forward to the city with foundations, whose architect and builder is God"* (Hebrews 11:10).

But listen to how God fuels the dream through the passions the Father created in Abraham. We read:

> *After this, the word of the Lord came to Abram in a vision: "Do not be afraid, Abram. I am your shield, your very great reward."*
>
> *But Abram said, "O Sovereign Lord, what can you give me since I remain childless and the one who will inherit my estate is Eliezer of Damascus?"*
>
> *And Abram said, "You have given me no children; so a servant in my household will be my heir." Then the word of the Lord came to him: "This man will not be your heir, but a son coming from your own body will be your heir."*
>
> *He took him outside and said, "Look up at the heavens and count the stars—if indeed you can count them." Then he said to him, "So shall your offspring be"* (Genesis 15:1-5).

At that moment Abraham probably started to get that crazy look in his eye— *"Hey Sarrrrahhh! Hello my little desert flower!"*

Sarah was thinking: *"You are wacky, Abe! You've been out in the field too long!"*

Abraham is the ancient "Juice Man" or Jack LaLane of his day. Suddenly, he's rejuvenated. He starts walking toward Sarah with a new sense of destiny.

The miracle of the story is that as unlikely as it sounded in the natural, Abraham believed God. When others were thinking about retiring and fading off into the sunset, his faith reignited a passion to see the fruition of a dream he thought had long since died. But God in His providence made it come alive again!

GO FOR THE GOLD!

The Lord delights in fulfilling the desires of our hearts in the process of pursuing His ultimate dream for our lives. Some people think that being a follower of Christ is boring and legalistic. I admit, sadly, that many Christians have been more vocal about what we are against than what we are for. But Jesus straightened out this notion when He declared: *"I have come that they might have life, and have it to the full"* (John 10:10).

I don't believe that God is sitting in a warehouse in heaven waiting for our catalog orders to be processed so He can shower us with our requests. In fact, the book of James reveals that some of our prayers are not answered because they are too self-centered. But, I do believe that we all have desires that God would find great pleasure in fulfilling simply because He loves blessing us while we're following the dream He has so graciously given.

_____▲_____

It is time to stir up the passion and purpose that lies dormant within—to take the lid off your dreams and believe God for something extraordinary.

When this message was preached in our church, we had over a hundred leaders dispersed throughout the building placing gold medals around the neck of every person in attendance. It was a visible reminder that there is a God-given dream in every heart.

Awaken the dream! Go for the gold!

TWO

PACE YOURSELF

Since we live by the Spirit
let us keep in step with the Spirit.
– GALATIANS 5:25

Our lives get in step with God...
by letting him set the pace.
– ROMANS 3:28 TM

I t's mind-boggling to think about the fact that there are over 6.9 billion people in this world and not one single individual has the same DNA.

You are uniquely made and there will never, ever be another you! God never runs out of creative power and doesn't try to duplicate people. He creates a treasure with every child who is born.

Take a close look at your family and you'll discover the uniqueness of each member. Believe it or not, every time you look into a mirror, you are gazing at a masterpiece!

As we learned in the last chapter, the Lord has placed a dream in your heart and has designed you for greatness.

When our oldest son was just a little boy, he turned to me and asked, *"Dad, was I born to be wild?"*

I smiled and responded, *"All signs point to YES!"* He was always doing something that would make us hold our breath.

One time he ran out of the house with a cape tied around his neck. My wife and I just turned our heads and winced as we waited for the crash!

————▲————

We all have a purpose for being here—and yours is distinct from anyone else on this planet.

"THE SCARCITY PRINCIPLE"

There is a law that might help illustrate the value God has placed on every person. It's called "the scarcity principle." I first heard of this from Pastor Tommy Barnett.

Economics teach us that the value of an object is determined by how rare it is. The scarcer the item, the greater its worth. For example, gas prices soar because of the threats of foreign oil being withheld or hurricanes closing down oil rigs at sea. The value of gold continues to escalate because its discovery is becoming increasingly rare.

The reason you are so valuable is because you are one of a kind. The Bible declares we have been *"fearfully and wonderfully made"* (Psalm 139:14).

I laughed when a friend said, "Some may be more *fearful* than *wonderful*," but God designed each of us to experience life fully—and He didn't make a mistake in the process. According to Scripture, *"We are God's masterpiece. He has created us anew in Christ Jesus, so we can do the good things he planned for us long ago"* (Ephesians 2:10 NLT).

She's Priceless!

Kerry Shook, Senior Pastor of Fellowship of the Woodlands, reminded me, through one of his messages, about a woman who lives in Paris.

She dwells in a room worth millions of dollars that is kept at a perfect 68 degrees Fahrenheit. She is protected behind bulletproof glass. Her soft brown eyes and mysterious smile have captivated countless people around the world. Her name: "The Mona Lisa"—a masterpiece painted by Leonardo da Vinci in the 16th century.

I've got to be honest. When I see replicas of The Mona Lisa, I think, "What's the big deal? She's just an ordinary looking gal with an ordinary smile."

It's a relatively small canvas painting. But The Mona Lisa is the most rare and valuable painting in the world. It is priceless!

This not only reveals how little I know about the value of art, it also unveils how often I undervalue the precious lives that surround me. The Mona Lisa is off the scale dollar wise because there is no monetary value high enough to replace an original.

This is also your story. You are one of a kind and

irreplaceable. And, only you can fulfill what God has placed in your heart.

Are you getting the picture? Pun intended!

DARE TO BELIEVE

There are bestsellers waiting to be written and songs hidden in hearts. There's a blank canvas waiting to become a masterpiece and epidemics crying out for relief. Justice is calling in the streets for anyone who will follow its voice. Emptiness is aching to be filled by someone who cares, and pain is screaming for comfort on a hurting planet.

―――――▲―――――

The world awaits men and women who are daring enough to believe God and the dream He has given them personally.

The best coaches have not yet risen to the top of their profession. The greatest Christian athletes have yet to become champions. Mankind will be introduced to yet another brilliant doctor who will discover a medical breakthrough.

All of these scenarios and more are waiting for a few dreamers who are daring enough to believe that we serve a miracle-working God. He still takes mere clay and creates treasures—and the Lord desires to do this in you and me.

There is a divine calling upon you to run your race

in a way that only you can—to the glory of God!

Friend, you've been given a lane in this life which has been specifically marked out for you. And the Lord designed you to step up and put your foot on the starting block. The gun has sounded and it's time to run!

God has gifted each of us with unique talents and passions. He has crafted and made us with different temperaments. Some are calm while others are excitable, but however He created you there is an exciting dream that is alive and waiting to be fanned into flame.

SHE DIDN'T LOOK BACK

In the first part of the fifteenth century a French peasant girl by the name of Joan of Arc was thirteen years of age when she sensed a call from God to save her country from the oppression of the English regime.

For her to obtain an audience with the rulers of that day is a story in and of itself. It wasn't long before she was in the presence of the most powerful men in France and she convinced them she was going to be the one who would lead their country to victory.

She had a firm conviction about the dream God gave her that caused armies to melt in her presence. Her dynamic influence was unmatched by any leader of the day.

On one occasion she called one of her generals and announced: *"I will lead the men over the wall."*

The general responded: *"Not a man will follow you."*

Joan of Arc confidently replied: *"I won't be looking back to see if they are following me."*

Talk about passion and getting in your lane, and not worrying about anyone else! She was not wasting valuable time looking back.

The men did follow her and she was initially victorious.

This determined woman had set a course and she was going to follow the vision God had placed in her heart.

Joan of Arc paid the ultimate sacrifice in the pursuit of her God-given dream. At nineteen years of age, she was burned at the stake for her cause.

Just before she died she gave this statement: *"Every man gives his life for what he believes, and every woman gives her life for what she believes. Sometimes people believe in little or nothing, and yet they give their lives to that little or nothing. One life is all we have; we live it and it is gone. But...to live without belief is more terrible than dying, even more terrible than dying young."*

Winston Churchill spoke of her, saying: *"Joan was a being so uplifted from the ordinary run of mankind that she finds no equal in a thousand years."*

It is recorded in history that judges and soldiers wept as she spoke to the crowd as she was tied to a stake, ready to be burned alive. Before she died, she forgave all of those who put her to death.

She cried out as the flames were beginning to lap at her feet. She asked for a symbol to be raised before her eyes. As she shouted out her request, *"Somebody get me a cross!"* there was an individual in the crowd who made a make-shift cross out of just two wooden sticks. It was elevated to eye level so she could focus on the Dream Giver.

Her final recorded word was, *"Jesus."*

The Author of life was completing the final chapter of her existence on this earth.

ONLY YOU

The writer of Hebrews says: *"Let us run with perseverance the race marked out for us. Let us fix our eyes on Jesus, the author and perfecter of our faith"* (Hebrews 12:1-2).

The apostle Paul ran with the same intensity and focus when he declared: *"For to me, to live is Christ and to die is gain"* (Philippians 1:21).

To die for Him would have been an upgrade!

————▲————

You and I each have a lane to run in and an individual pace to keep. Only you can run your race.

- Only you can be a husband or wife to your spouse.

- Only you can be a parent to your child.
- Only you can choose to grow spiritually and mentally.
- Only you can choose to follow the Spirit's leadings in your race.

God directs each of us differently and we all have been assigned a specific path in this journey of life. So it is your responsibility to run and pace yourself as God directs you! Be reminded once again: *"Our lives get in step with God...by letting him set the pace"* (Romans 3:28).

"THE GREAT COACH"

Regardless of what you may think, you have unbelievable potential. But it is not enough just to believe this, you need someone to coax these possibilities out of you. There is much more inside than raw talent, and you have the opportunity for the Holy Spirit, "The Great Coach," to reside within and do a supernatural work.

————▲————

The Spirit wants to help you achieve the right spiritual pace.

Too many people are trying to achieve their purpose without any divine conditioning. Jesus doesn't just want to be *with* you, God's Son promises: *"I will ask the Father, and he will give you another Counselor [Coach] to be with you forever—the Spirit of truth. The world cannot accept Him, because it neither sees Him nor knows Him. But you know Him, for He lives with you and will be in you"* (John 14:16-17).

When Jesus was crucified on the cross He declared He was going to rise again—and He did! Hallelujah! Then He ascended to His Father and sent the Person of the Holy Spirit to dwell in each and every believer.

I love the thought-provoking question coined by the beverage company that makes Gatorade®. They ask in a heart-pumping fashion: *"Is it in you?"* During the commercial, viewers see athletes drinking this thirst-quenching product. Gatorade® gets so deep into their system that it begins to flow out of their pores. They are sweating Fierce Grape and Riptide Rush as the question is asked, *"Is it in you?"*

We can ask ourselves a similar question: "Is He in me?"

Spiritually, whatever is inside will come out of your very pores. What you are drinking in to satisfy your thirst for God will be evident to everyone. When the Holy Spirit is operating in a person's life, there is proof of passion, and tides of love, joy, and peace will come pouring out of you.

Faithfulness, gentleness, and kindness will freely flow.

Filled to Overflowing

People are breaking apart at the seams because of self-induced deficiencies. But the Lord wants to be your Life Coach as you run your race on this planet.

Perhaps the question should be, "Are you tired? Are you worn out? Are you weary of doing life in your own strength? Are you stressed out and worried? Are you burdened with sorrow or guilt?"

Invite the Holy Spirit to do a work in you to renew your energy and vitality. He wants to fill you to such an extent that you can't help but be poured out to others.

You may wonder, "Well, how can I get started?" Begin by simply asking Him—praying: *"Father, begin to coach me today by the leadership of Your Holy Spirit and help me to do what is right. Fill me with Your power, in Jesus name. Amen."*

In the natural we are going to become fatigued and wear out, but the Bible promises: *"They that wait upon the Lord shall renew their strength; they shall mount up with wings as eagles; they shall run, and not be weary; and they shall walk, and not faint"* (Isaiah 40:31 KJV).

Now that you have invited Him to guide you in this race of life, what the Holy Spirit begins to lead you toward may at first seem insignificant. For example, the Spirit may begin to impress upon you to write a short note or call someone who is hurting and encourage them.

You may wonder, "Is that the Holy Spirit placing this in my mind?"

Absolutely. He might motivate you to forgive an individual who has wronged you, or He may ask you to walk the extra mile for a colleague you don't particularly like. He may challenge you to confess a deep dark secret to a trusted friend. He may ask you to give away a possession you prize, or He may call you to share your dream with someone who can pray with and partner with you to see it come true.

New Direction

In the case of Joan of Arc, the first thing she was instructed to do by the Holy Spirit was *"Go to church!"* It was her first step on her path toward changing the course of history.

———▲———

Whatever He coaches you to do,
follow through—and you will begin to see
exciting new levels of spiritual growth.

If you are bored, tired, and frustrated, it may be because you have been keeping pace to the beat of your own music. It's time to let the Holy Spirit lead and for you to get in step with what He wants to do in and through you.

Stop spinning your wheels. Welcome the Holy

Spirit to begin this work in your life. He will challenge you to exercise the core qualities that should be in every Christian—love, joy, peace, patience, kindness, goodness, faithfulness, gentleness, and self-control.

––––––––––▲––––––––––

When the Spirit begins to do His work, you will begin to discover who you are meant to be.

PACE-SETTING PRINCIPLES

Where do we begin? Here are three practical pace setting principles that will get you started:

First: Listen to the Coach

We cannot afford to go through this race of life without the advice and guidance of the Holy Spirit. The top football players in the world have someone to thank for their success. It's more than "MOM" when they score a touchdown. They also have a coach to thank.

To help them reach their maximum potential there was a mentor—good or bad, right or wrong—who helped shape their skills and talents. This is the person who drew the best out of them, who helped define who they are today.

You may complain, *"Well, I never had a good coach."*

Perhaps you didn't like their methods or personality, but I'm sure they contributed to the development of your character—even if you were taught what *not* to do. So thank them anyway!

Raw talent without a coachable spirit is a disaster waiting to happen. We see it all the time in professional sports with super-stars who won't play team ball.

The mark of a great athlete is that they never stop growing. You can have all the talent in the world, but you will only reach a certain level of performance unless you accept the help of a seasoned coach. I like to call it "Gaining the Advantage."

It's not my own thought, but is found in the Bible. Jesus gave us the secret to successful Christian living by saying: *"It is to your advantage that I go away; for if I do not go away, the Helper [Coach] will not come to you; but if I depart, I will send Him to you"* (John 16:7 NKJV).

"YOU ARE A SOMEBODY"

When I was called by God into full time Christian service, in the beginning I felt inferior to every pastor I could think of because I grew up in an unchurched family and I wasn't surrounded by high-profile ministers.

Since there were few spiritual coaches to guide me along the way, I felt I wasn't going to be as effective for the Kingdom as other people.

Then one day the Holy Spirit illuminated my mind; He impressed upon me that He wanted to reside and partner with me to produce the most capable "Me" I could possibly be.

The Lord said, *"This is your lane Dave, and I want you to run."*

Don't look around at others and be discouraged. When you think you are a "Nobody," the Holy Spirit will come along side and whisper to your heart, saying, "You are a Somebody."

When you feel down and out and there's not another ounce of energy to give, He speaks and a supernatural wind fills your sail—and you don't even know where the strength came from.

At that moment you begin to understand. You lift your eyes to heaven and exclaim: *"My help comes from the Lord. He's my strength, He's my life. He is my everything."*

If you have been at a standstill in your faith, ask the Holy Spirit to breathe new power into your life. He will infuse you with unexpected strength. You may be afraid and confused, trying to figure out how your circumstances are going to resolve themselves. Stop and ask the Holy Spirit to give you wisdom, understanding, and to show you the path to follow.

HOW THE LORD SPEAKS

To know how to stay "on pace" with the Lord, start reading the playbook! The Bible is God's perfect instruction manual for running in your lane of life.

You may say, *"It's just a book!"* No, the Bible is

God's breath. You are inviting the wind of His Spirit to flow through you when you read the Bible. You are not just studying the text when you open the pages, God is studying you! As you read, He is sharpening your mind and conditioning your heart for peak performance on the course He has called you to run. We are told: *"All Scripture is inspired by God and is useful to teach us what is true and to make us realize what is wrong in our lives. It corrects us when we are wrong and teaches us to do what is right"* (2 Timothy 3:16 NLT).

————▲————

Meditating on God's Word will help you recognize the Spirit's voice.

Some people, unaware of how we hear from the Lord, say, *"God never speaks to me."*

Yes, He does!

Personally, the Lord doesn't speak to me audibly. As I am driving down a highway, I don't hear, *"Now, Dave you're going to have to turn right up here."*

But let me tell you how He *does* communicate. As I read His Word, divine principles are etched on my mind. Then, when a situation blocks my way, I have the wisdom to know which direction to turn. He quickens my spirit by something that I've read in the past.

If you have nothing in the bank, you're not going to have the resources you need when financial trouble hits. This is why I am telling you to bank God's Word in your inner man. Study, meditate, and spend time with the playbook every day of your life.

Second: Practice, Practice, Practice!

Just do it!

You can dress for the race and have all of the Bibles, highlighters, Concordances, and other Christian paraphernalia, but if you don't apply what the Holy Spirit has spoken to your life, you are simply a poser. It's like a runner buying all of the athletic gear and sitting in the living room eating potato chips while watching television. It is one thing to read *Runner's Magazine*, but it's quite another to put the shoes on and hit the pavement!

The Bible cautions: *"Do not merely listen to the word, and so deceive yourselves. Do what it says"* (James 1:22).

Today, start running the race!

DON'T BECOME DISTRACTED

We can get so busy doing life that it passes us by! This is illustrated by the story of Martha in the Bible. When Jesus came to visit two sisters in Bethany, Scripture records: *"Now as they were traveling along, He entered a village; and a woman named Martha welcomed Him into her home. She had a sister called Mary, who was seated at the Lord's feet, listening to*

His word" (Luke 10:38-39 NASB).

They were excited because Jesus was their guest. I can see Him walking up on the porch and knocking on the door. With joy, these two sisters led Him into their home.

Can you imagine the thoughts racing through their minds? *"The Messiah is in our house!"*

Martha's mentality was, *"Everything has to be perfect!"* While Mary thought, *"I can't wait to hear what He has to say!"*

------▲------

We get sidetracked trying to create absolutely ideal scenarios, yet they seldom arrive.

There is never a perfect time to sit at His feet and listen—so a few things may need to remain undone in order to establish the right priorities.

Martha worries, gets uptight and full of stress, while Mary just sits there in peace, receiving from the Lord.

Mary sat down at the feet of Jesus as soon as He walked in the door. She didn't want to miss a word He said. Then there's Martha in the kitchen clanging pots and pans. She is not a happy homemaker! Moans can be heard seeping into the sitting room where Jesus and Mary are talking. You can hear Martha; *"I sure could use a little help in here! I'd like to be a part of the conversation too!"*

Mary and Jesus are having a great time conversing,

as Martha stews in the kitchen. Every time Mary laughs, it shoots a dagger into the overworked Martha. Something trivial sends Martha over the edge causing her to storm out of the kitchen in anger. "That's it, I've had enough!"

Martha marched in and interrupted the conversation in mid-sentence. The Bible says: *"Martha was distracted with all her preparations; and she came up to Him and said, 'Lord, do you not care that my sister has left me to do all the serving alone? Then, tell her to help me!'"* (Luke 10:40 NASB).

WHAT REALLY COUNTS?

Allow me to offer a word of advice. Don't be like Martha, who comes charging in to reprimand the Creator of the universe: *"Jesus, tell Mary to lend a hand. I want to be in here with You, but I'm too busy trying to get things organized!"*

I often meet people who make this excuse: *"Let me get my life in order first, then I will come to God."*

According to Jesus' response to Martha, this kind of thinking is backwards. Scripture tells us: *"But the Lord answered and said to her 'Martha, Martha, you are worried and bothered about so many things"* (verse 41).

What is she so anxious over? The food, the dishes, the temperature of the oven? Martha has all these things churning in her mind, and it's overwhelming.

Then Jesus tells her: *"But only one thing is necessary, for Mary has chosen the good part, which shall not be taken away from her"* (verse 42).

In other words, Mary has opted for the one thing that really counts. She is sitting at the feet of Jesus.

Martha had everything wrong. She couldn't move ahead because of her self-induced distractions.

It is easy to overbook our day and crowd out what is essential.

————▲————

We must learn to prioritize our time for the most important thing, which is being in the presence of the Dream Maker.

Third: Run Your Race!

Never compare yourself with others, but run *your* best possible race.

Peter was in his lane and Jesus was giving him a few coaching tips concerning how he was going to suffer great pain in his Christian race. In fact, Jesus let Peter know he wouldn't like where he was being sent.

The Lord stated: *"I tell you the truth, when you were younger you dressed yourself and went where you wanted; but when you are old you will stretch out your hands, and someone else will dress you and lead you where you do not want to go"* (John 21:18)

The Lord mentioned this *"to indicate the kind of death by which Peter would glorify God. Then He said to him, 'Follow me!'"* (verse 19).

This is unusual motivation. To paraphrase, Jesus says: *"Listen Peter, you're in your lane, but let me tell you what's about to happen as you travel through."*

Peter probably replied, "Yeah, tell me. Tell me! There are going to be kingdoms and power and all of these great things. Right?"

Jesus responds: *"Well, actually, I want you to keep pace with where the Holy Spirit is taking you but you're not going to like it."*

Peter says: *"What? Wait! Whoa!"*

Jesus concludes: *"Just follow me."*

"GET OVER IT!"

Perhaps you've been there. Everything is smooth sailing until the Lord gives you a difficult assignment. Then all of a sudden, you don't want to run the race which He has marked out.

———▲———

As long as everything is going well in our lives, we are delighted to follow God. But when we start experiencing a few struggles, we have a tendency to start comparing our life with others.

Jesus was telling Peter, *"I'm taking you where you may not want to go, but if you get over it, you will find*

48

out it is for the best. So follow me."

Because of this statement Peter started looking over his shoulder trying to see what kind of race everyone else was running. He turned and saw the disciple whom Jesus loved (John), which may have been a little irritating. When Peter saw John, he asked: *"Lord, what about him?"* (verse 21).

Jesus answered: *"If I want him to remain alive until I return, what is that to you? You must follow me"* (verse 22). Wow! Jesus sternly warns Peter to mind his own race. *"Just follow Me. I have a greater purpose planned that you do not understand."*

What Peter didn't know at the time was that he would become a builder—the foundation on which the church would be established. Jesus told him: *"For this was not revealed to you by man, but by my Father in heaven. And I tell you that you are Peter, and on this rock I will build my church, and the gates of Hades will not overcome it"* (Matthew 16:17-18).

In essence, the Lord was revealing: *"Peter, you are going to be magnificent. You may not like it at first, but trust and follow Me."*

WHAT IS YOUR SPECIAL MISSION?

The context of my life is centered in leading people in a growing relationship with Christ. Because I pastor a church, I listen to podcasts of some of the greatest leaders in the Christian faith. I want to learn and grow, so I look to them for inspiration.

Then one day, listening to Bill Hybles, I understood, "*I can never be a Bill Hybels, but I can be the best Dave Ansell I can possibly be under the power of the Holy Spirit.*"

Wayne Cordeiro is an awesome pastor in Hawaii. I love to visit his church for more reasons than one (location, location, location). I love his heart and what he's doing for the Lord, but I could never be a Wayne Cordeiro. He has his special lane in which to run.

I can't be Joel Osteen and this is okay with me. Joel has his specific mission.

Tommy Barnett motivates me like few people can, but again, I could never walk in his shoes.

Andy Stanley, Rick Warren, Greg Laurie, Ed Young, and so many more have unique callings, but I don't need to be distracted and confused with what is going on in their lives. I have a responsibility to remain focused on the mission God has given exclusively to me—and remind myself to stay fixed on the race lane the Lord has placed me in.

ARRIVE IN STYLE!

Getting caught up in a comparison game reminds me of a story that an old preacher named Clovis Chapel used to tell about a steamboat race on the Mississippi River. Two paddleboats were heading down the river at the same time when they got the idea that one wanted to race the other. So the contest was on!

Suddenly, they were heaping coals on the fire to make the steam. One boat edged out in front of the other and was just about to take a good lead when it ran out of coal.

What did they do? They started throwing all their cargo on the fire, stoking it into a huge flame.

It worked! They pulled ahead and won the race. But unfortunately, they burned up all their expensive cargo in the process.

When we start comparing ourselves with others, and attempt to run a race that was not designed for us, all we're doing is burning up the precious cargo that God has entrusted us to deliver to a needy world. You may win the race—and outdistance a Joel Osteen or a Tommy Barnett—but you haven't arrived at your destiny in the way God planned.

The Lord placed something inside you that needs to be delivered in style—*your style!*

Run your race. And, let God set the pace!"

THREE

R.U.N. FOR LIFE

*Let us run with perseverance
the race marked out for us.*

– HEBREWS 12:1

There are several things I hate intruding my day.

I don't like to stop and read junk mail, or to answer the phone when it's a telemarketer.

I dislike walking through the mall and being accosted by the sales people in the center aisle kiosks. You know what I'm referring to. They lay in wait for passers by: *"Sir, do you mind if I ask you a question?"* Then they try to rub sea salt on my hands or place a bean bag on my neck. I also dislike having the guys from the cell phone hut track me down and ask me what service I use, or how much my plan costs.

I don't like to stop working on my computer when a pop-up indicates, "New update. Do it now, or remind me later." I always click "later."

Finally, I loathe stopping for gasoline—especially when fuel costs more than kids' braces!

I laughed when late-night comedian Jay Leno said,

"Gas prices continue to rise. At the gas station near my house they have a slot for your bank card and one right next to it for your 401K."

Of course, refueling my car is a necessity of life. But I don't like playing twenty questions with the computer on the gas pump. Credit or Debit? Car wash? Zip Code? What grade? Do you want a receipt? Sorry—see attendant!

The truth is, on our journey there are times we don't want to stop to refuel spiritually. But unless we do we will end up stranded on the side of the road with only fumes remaining in the tank.

----------▲----------

If you need stamina to reach your God-given dream, you must stop and fill up at the Divine Service Station.

There are those who like to play the "How far can I make it on empty?" game. The fuel gauge on the dash board has been reading empty all day, but when one of the passengers points out that you need some gas, you reply, "Don't worry. We are good for another twenty miles."

There are far too many who are misreading the fuel indicator of their spiritual life, believing, "It's on empty, but I can make another trip. I know my limits."

Then we find ourselves depleted and complain, "What's wrong with me? I just don't have any joy in my life. I'm so stressed."

Spiritually Depleted

I want to talk to you candidly about the importance of refueling because this was once my problem.

Several years ago I found myself in the middle of a spiritual rat race, trying to keep up with both the pace of the church and my life. I was allowing my days to be dictated by everything but the Holy Spirit.

When this happens, we are not consistently "topping off our tank" spiritually and we become sitting ducks for the enemy to come in and siphon any ounce of life left in our soul.

I was left stranded on the side of the road feeling frustrated, and depressed—not wanting to go another mile, at my wit's end because I knew I had nothing more to give. It seemed like every area of my life was running on empty.

When you neglect refueling spiritually, you start taking from every other energy source of your life. Before long, your mental and emotional capacity takes a nose dive. Your ability to deal with people and to love your family diminishes, not to mention loving God. Your life begins to crack like the ground in a parched desert that hasn't seen rain in years.

"Catch Me When I Fall"

I'm not the type of individual who picks up the phone and just starts calling people randomly. You know, "Hey! Hello! How are you doing?"

While I have very close friends, I wasn't sure they would be able to help me through this valley. And at first I hesitated even sharing my feelings with them.

But finally, in desperation, I phoned a friend who advised me to call another individual who had gone through a similar experience. So, with little emotion, I dialed the number.

The friendly voice on the other end responded, "Dave, what can I do for you?"

He was so generous, so kind—I could hear the love of God flowing through him.

Choosing my words carefully, I began, "If I can use an analogy, I will tell you."Then I admitted, "I just need somebody to be underneath me to catch me when I fall. Because I'm letting go."

Again, he asked, "How can I help?"

I responded, "Just give me a net to fall into."

Immediately he said, "I've got the net under you, buddy. Let go!"

I thought, "Wow, that's all I needed is for somebody to tell me 'Your going to make it!'"

That same week my wife and I decided to book a flight, to receive some solid counsel. It was the beginning of an awesome refueling process. No, it didn't happen overnight, but I soon found myself on the road to revitalization.

Getting the "drive" back for life and ministry was incredibly refreshing. I realized that I had been doing things in my own strength and capacity for too long.

STOP PUSHING

It makes no sense to struggle through life dependent solely upon ourselves when we have divine power available to us. It's like purchasing a brand new car with this beefed-up engine and inviting all of your friends to take a ride. Excited, they all come over and pile in, but you put your hands on the back bumper and push the car down the street. They would think you were crazy!

But many of us live this way every day. We have the power of the Holy Spirit available to us but we decide to push through in our own strength. We may eventually make it to our destination, but we are too exhausted to enjoy it when we finally arrive.

———————▲———————

If you have to force yourself out of bed, push yourself to work every morning, or make yourself spend time with your family, it's time to be refreshed and refueled.

On life's journey there will always be pressure and tension, but if you try to cope with the pressure and tension without a vital spiritual relationship with God, you are going to find yourself on the side of the road, empty and broken down.

SURRENDER TO WHAT YOU CAN'T SEE

I trust you will allow the Lord to refuel your soul today. Paul prayed that: *"You will be made complete with all the fullness of life and power that comes from God"* (Ephesians 3:19 NLT).

The word "filled" in Greek actually means to be *continuously* filled. It's not just adding more fuel when you're on empty, but fullness becomes a life-style. Wouldn't it be great to have a bottomless tank that never runs dry? We do, through Christ. We just need to tap into Him to have real power for living!

———▲———

Forget about yesterday and tomorrow, you must be refueled daily. This is what brings joy and vitality.

I love the song, "Whatever You're Doing" by the band, Sanctus Real. The lyrics include:

> *Whatever you're doing inside of me*
> *It feels like chaos, somehow there's peace*
> *It's hard to surrender to what I can't see*
> *But I'm giving in to something heavenly.*

The song continues: *"It's time to face up; clean this old house. Time to breath in and let everything out."*
Amen!

The Necessary Ingredients

As believers, we need to develop a plan for keeping our spiritual tank full. Everything in our lives—physically, emotionally, mentally, and spiritually — is connected to this life source. If our relationship with God is not in sync, our whole life is playing out of tune.

If I were to take a survey and ask, *"Do you have a plan that you practice daily for spiritual health?"* The majority of folks would have to sit back and admit, *"I really don't. I want to, but I'm more random in my approach to spiritual things."*

This was my problem. I was an active pastor, yet I didn't have a spiritual growth plan. I wasn't refueling myself daily. Instead, I was operating without rhyme or reason. When I saw that the gauge was indicating half empty I would say, "Wow, I better start filling up." But I usually decided to see how close to "E" I could go before getting back in that groove again of searching for God and asking Him for His infilling power in my life.

Please don't make the mistake of thinking you can refuel "on the run."

Some people say, *"I think about God all day long."* Well, that's wonderful. But somewhere you have to stop long enough for the refueling process to take place, and for God to fill you with the energy and divine nutrition you need to handle what you are about to face.

We may not know what is best for our system, but He does.

A PLAN FOR RENEWAL

As we address this issue, I believe it will be helpful to release any guilt you may have concerning your present devotional deficiencies. This usually springs from our belief that every other Christian has an incredible daily fellowship time with God. From my experience, for most people this is not the case.

————▲————

In today's fast-paced world, everyone struggles to carve out the time and establish habits which lead to a vibrant relationship with God.

During my spiritual drought, the Lord helped me develop a plan that led me back to the land of the living. While in this dry season of my life I made a choice to get in the best physical, emotional, and spiritual shape I could. This required making some drastic changes. But before any radical decision was made that would affect our whole family, I needed sound judgment.

One day while I was running, the Lord impressed upon me a plan for renewal. It was a simple acronym spelling out the word R.U.N., which stands for Rejoice, Unveil, and Name It.

As I began to journal and explore these words, I introduced a pattern into my life and it began to help me restore that which I had lost. Since that time, the ministry team at our church has put much into what has become a Bible reading and journaling plan I want to share with you.

It simply comes from what God did in my life and the rest of our staff as we embarked on this adventure together.

ACCEPT THE CHALLENGE

I've heard Rick Warren say: *"Inspiration without information leads to frustration."* With that in mind, let's get practical about how to R.U.N. for LIFE.

This is not a program or a campaign; it is designed to be a lifestyle, something you can do every day. I want to personally challenge you to give it a try for 90 days.

Sincerely try to practice these principles faithfully. Then, after you become familiar with the journaling experience you may want to tweak this model to better fit you personally. The major objective is to find a daily routine that works for you.

A THREE-PART PLAN

R.U.N for LIFE has three parts: The first deals with our daily attitude and prayer. Second is a daily Bible reading plan. Third, you will learn to track your exercise and diet for the day.

To learn more about the resource materials

available, including reminder bracelets and journals, the contact information can be found at the end of this book.

When I began this exercise, I purchased a blank journal and wrote the letters R.U.N. vertically on the left page.

You should space the letters an equal distance apart to give you room to write under each one.

This is the first step of the plan. It will help align your attitude as you spend a few minutes praying and jotting down some thoughts to get your day started on the right track.

Remember, the R.U.N. acronym stands for Rejoice, Unveil, and Name It. You can write these words in your journal to remind yourself as you're noting your thoughts.

R—REJOICE

I want to challenge you to start your day with thoughts of REJOICING! When your eyes open in the morning, your first step is to become involved in a prayer and attitude plan.

One of two options exists concerning our outlook. We can have the attitude: *"Good God, it's morning!"* But how much better to say: *"Good morning God!"*

Start by affirming the Word and declare: *"This is the day the Lord has made; let us rejoice and be glad in it!"* (Psalm 118:24). Or, *"Rejoice in the Lord always. I will say it again: Rejoice!"* (Philippians 4:4).

Obviously, God wants us to rejoice—or He wouldn't have repeated it twice!

_____▲_____

If you really want to see changes on your daily journey, it all begins with attitude. This leads to affections, the things you love, and affections lead to attributes, the things that you are.

A negative outlook causes you to engage in activities that aren't in your best interest. Feeling "down" results in self-destructive behavior, and sooner or later this will take it's toll. The exterior of your life will begin to unravel and show how depleted you are on the inside.

The Bible tells us we are to take on the attitude of Christ. Can you imagine if the roles were reversed and Christ were to take on our attitude? In golfing terms, we would all be off the fairway and "in the rough."

We have a choice in what we want to focus our attention on. As Paul writes: *"Whatever is true, whatever is noble, whatever is right, whatever is pure, whatever is lovely, whatever is admirable—if anything is excellent or praiseworthy—think about such things"* (Philippians 4:8).

Rejoicing encompasses much more than an attitude; it is an invitation for God's presence to flow through your life. Why? Because the Lord inhabits the praises of His people (Psalm 22:3).

If you want the power of God surging through you in a fresh way, start praising! Start rejoicing!

————▲————

*When we fill our minds with praiseworthy
thoughts, we are washing out all the negativity
that gets trapped in our soul.*

There is amazing power in praise, which we can experience in at least three ways:

1. Through praise-filled SONGS
God's presence fills us when we lift our voices to Him in song. It is not necessary to be in a church worship service to sing unto the Lord. Find a place alone and let Him hear the song of your heart.

2. Through praise-filled LIPS
We are not to let any unwholesome words leave our mouth. Anyone can be negative, but we need to speak with grace and express with our lips how great and loving our God is—and how blessed we are as His children. We are to give thanks in all circumstances because God is Good.

3. Through praise-filled MINDS
Our minds are the filtering system to our soul. If they are cluttered or filled with garbage or litter, the flow of God's life-giving Word will be impaired.

We can exercise physically, but if we are not eating properly, our bodies will be depleted of vital nutrition. The same applies to our thoughts. It really matters what information enters our minds and what dominates our thinking throughout the day.

If we allow our thoughts to create negative scenarios that may never happen, we will be wasting precious energy on things that will delay us from reaching our dreams.

Find what is good—and think on these things!

U—UNVEIL

The tendency with journaling is to write what you *think* should be written—all the things you are doing right. We leave everything else out in case someone might peek inside and discover our innermost thoughts. We may also be thinking this is what God *wants* to hear. But we are not helping ourselves and certainly not impressing the Lord by filling up pages with disingenuous entries.

As I told our congregation, to UNVEIL is to get REAL with yourself and get RAW with God! In other words, total transparency.

We can take our lead from King David as he poured his soul out to the Lord in both good times and bad. We appreciate David's life because of his willingness to be honest regarding what was on his heart. As he wrote: *"You want complete honesty, so teach me true wisdom"* (Psalm 51:6 CEV).

THE SHOTGUN!

When I was in high school, I was invited to house-sit for my boss. He generously told me, "You can enjoy the whole house. Make yourself at home."

He and his wife were going on vacation for two weeks and they wanted someone responsible to take care of things while they were gone. Their faith in me boosted my ego. I thought I was the cream of the crop, and the best of the best. But, on the other hand, maybe they couldn't find anyone else!

The first couple of nights I really enjoyed having the television and refrigerator all to myself. That was the extent of enjoying the whole house. By the third day, however, I was getting a little bored with the routine, so I started investigating—some might call it snooping around!

I made my way to the bedroom, started rummaging through the closets, and there in plain sight was a shotgun calling my name. I thought to myself, "I need this weapon to protect the valuables of this residence."

I picked up the gun and slid back the wooden piece attached to the chamber. For those unfamiliar with guns, I had just unintentionally loaded the shotgun with a shell.

As I started to sit on the bed to take a closer look at the weapon, instantly I realized that this was not a normal bed—it was a waterbed and I lost my balance.

"Why didn't they tell me?" I thought.

As I was falling back, the shotgun blasted and nearly hit my leg. It scared the living daylights out of me!

The good news was, the bullet missed both my leg and the waterbed. The bad news however, was I had just shot a hole in my boss's custom cabinets that he had built into the wall!

I freaked out! *"Oh Lord, help me!"* And I started to think, *"How in the world am I going to fix this. It's just blown, shattered, it's gone!"*

---------▲---------

I was picking up pieces, saying, "I'm dead. I'm fired. I'm finished."

Quickly, I placed the shotgun back where it belonged.

After a sleepless night, the next day I called a friend. *"Listen,"* I said nervously, *"Your good with woodwork aren't you?"*

With some hesitation, *"Uhhhh—pretty good"* he replied. But when he came over, he admitted, *"I'm not that good, Dave!"*

We worked for several days on the cabinet, with practically no improvement. So, after two weeks of agony, I had to come to grips with reality, thinking, *"How am I ever going to tell him that I did this."*

First, I would have to admit that I was snooping in his closet and found the gun. Perhaps I could imply, *"There was a burglar in the house and I was looking for a gun or anything to protect your valuables and he ran by me and I missed him. Thank God I missed him! I am okay though."*

Trust me, such thoughts—and many others—raced through my mind.

The two weeks passed and as the owners were pulling into the driveway, I was praying, *"Oh dear God help me! Save me Jesus!"* It was amazing how spiritual I became.

As they walked in the door, I calmly asked, *"How was your vacation?"*

The husband responded, *"It was fabulous. We are so relaxed."*

I immediately thought, *"Well, that's about to change!"*

Then I blurted out, *"I shot a hole in your cabinet."*

Startled, he replied, *"What? Huh?"*

I walked him into his bedroom with my head hanging low and pointed, while repeating myself in a mumbled tone, *"I shot a hole in your cabinet."*

He was stunned for just a moment and then the laughter began. This was music to my ears because I was still alive and to my knowledge, I still had a job.

Then he added, *"You're an idiot!"*

And at that moment I couldn't have agreed more!

On that day I learned the valuable lesson that honesty is always the best policy and confession is good for the soul.

TOTAL TRANSPARENCY

King David caused much more damage than I caused with my shotgun debacle. The guilt that he felt after an affair with the wife of one of his most loyal military officers must have been overwhelming. If you are unfamiliar with the story, check it out in Second Samuel chapter eleven. The more David tried to cover up his sin, the worse it became.

As you will discover, someone ended up dead and the woman he had an adulterous affair with gave birth to a child—and the baby died.

It was brutal. David tried to cover all this up, but a prophet came along, asking, "Hey David, what's going on here?"

David replies, "Oh nothing. Absolutely nothing."

Finally, the prophet gets to the bottom of the matter and David begins to UNVEIL his heart to God. The prayer is recorded in Psalm 51: *"Create in me a pure heart, O God, and renew a steadfast spirit within me. Do not cast me from your presence or take your Holy Spirit from me"* (verses 10-11).

David came clean because of the damage he had caused. And, when we confess our faults and are honest before the Lord, He always responds with love and compassion.

Perhaps you are worn out and exhausted from carrying heavy burdens from your past mistakes. Once and for all, tell God about it and ask Him to remove the guilt and shame.

What you unveil may be as serious as David's error, but you can also include victories that are taking place. Don't hesitate to record joys, your gratitude to the Lord, or document your spiritual growth. Whatever it is, make it real.

N—NAME IT

In your journal, write out what you want God to do

in your life—for today, for the week, or in your future. Be specific in your requests and let the Lord know exactly what you are praying for.

Jesus says: *"If you get your life from Me and My Words live in you, ask whatever you want. It will be done for you"* (John 15:7 NLV).

In most cases we are timid, and pray too small. In the words of God's Son: *"Until now you have not asked for anything in My name. Ask and you will receive. Then your joy will be full"* (John 16:24 NLV).

What do you desire from your heavenly Father? Go ahead and NAME IT!

James says: *"You do not have, because you do not ask God"* (James 4:2 NIV).

Before we go jumping to conclusions about NAME IT, I am not suggesting that we ask God to fill our pockets with selfish living. In fact, the following verse reads: *"When you ask, you do not receive, because you ask with wrong motives, that you may spend what you get on your pleasures"* (verse 3 NIV).

We are wasting our time if we ask God to sponsor a selfish life. But for the life centered in Christ, nothing is impossible!

YOUR BIBLE READING PLAN

Part two of your R.U.N. for LIFE journal is the Bible reading plan.

There are many wonderful options available in Christian book stores or on the Internet, but in the journal we offer to our home church there are four separate tracks:

- A 31- day track—for those who want to give it a trial run at a jogging pace.

- A 61-day track—that takes people on a journey through the highlights of the Bible.

- A 90-day RUN—that guides readers through the New Testament in chronological order and includes the book of Proverbs.

- A one-year Marathon RUN—taking participants through the entire Bible in chronological order in 365 days.

Each reading plan takes about fifteen minutes of your time. (Note: More information on this is available at www.firstfamilychurch.net)

Why is it so imperative that we meditate on the Word? The Bible tells us: *"Blessed is the man who does not walk in the counsel of the wicked or stand in the way of sinners or sit in the seat of mockers. But his delight is in the law of the Lord, and on his law he meditates day and night. He is like a tree planted by streams of water, which yields its fruit in season and whose leaf does not wither. Whatever he does prospers"* (Psalms 1:1-3).

71

Add L.I.F.E.

On the pages of your journal which include your Bible reading plan, let me recommend that you write the acronym, L.I.F.E., vertically down the margin.

The Letter "L" stands for LIFT a verse.

As you are reading the Word, there will be something that pops up and grabs your attention. I like to keep a pen in my hand as I read and underline every verse that stands out to me. At the end of the reading time, I look back at the verse(s) highlighted and I choose one or two that seem to speak to me the most. I then write them in the journal word for word and jot down the reference. This is called LIFTING a verse.

This is kind of like shoplifting—only legal and much more productive! You need to view the verse that attracted your attention as a gift from the Holy Spirit.

This is God's primary way of talking with us, so it's incredible when we realize these are messages from the Lord that help us pursue the dream He has placed in our hearts.

"Let the word of Christ dwell in you richly" (Colossians 3:16).

The letter "I" stands for ILLUSTRATE.

The passage(s) you highlight won't do you any good until you put them into practice. Otherwise, it will be like having a treadmill at home that has become a towel rack! It's time to ILLUSTRATE that verse in your own words. What does it mean to you personally? Write out your thoughts.

Scripture tells us: *"Do what God's teaching says; when you only listen and do nothing, you are fooling yourselves. Those who hear God's teaching and do nothing are like people who look at themselves in a mirror. They see their faces and then go away and quickly forget what they looked like"* (James 1:22-24 NCV).

If you practice this consistently for one year you will have at least 365 verses that have been illustrated through your mind, into your heart, and onto the written page.

———————▲———————

How many verses have gone through your spirit in previous years? For me, sadly, nowhere near this amount. This exercise makes the Word come alive.

When you have finished ILLUSTRATING the verse(s), there is one final entry to be made in the Bible reading plan. Take a moment and TITLE the verse(s) that you just ILLUSTRATED. On the top of the page give your entry a name that will help you remember the verse that you just "worked out" with.

The letter "F" in L.I.F.E. stands for FOOD intake.

The final portion of the journal has to do with our physical health.

I am not a nutritionist. In fact, I struggle with this as

much as anyone else, but we have a responsibility to put healthy fuel into our bodies. We have all heard the statement, *"You are what you eat."* Friend, if this is true, I must be a walking burrito!

What we take into our body contributes to our mood patterns, energy levels, creativity, stress barriers, and it even affects our spiritual lives.

The number one cause of death in America is heart disease. It has held this position for years. Many believe this is because we live in a culture that promotes high fat and high cholesterol food.

It's interesting that some people are petrified to fly for fear of the plane crashing. Others won't swim in the ocean because of their fear of sharks. Yet, we don't seem to be one bit afraid of those fat-saturated, cholesterol-loaded, artery-clogging fries!

—————▲—————

We need to have a serious talk with ourselves concerning our eating habits.

The Bible asks: *"Do you not know that your body is a temple where the Holy Spirit lives? The Spirit is in you and is a gift from God. You are no longer your own. God paid a great price for you. So use your body to honor God"* (1 Corinthians 6:19-20 CEV).

Your physical body is the vehicle through which God operates to accomplish the purpose for which you were created. Health and wholeness offer the Lord the opportunity to use us in ways that would be limited if we disregard our physical well being. We are not honoring our Creator with our whole life if we make poor choices regarding food and nutrition.

There are plenty of dietary programs that can assist your particular needs, but I want to simply suggest that you take a moment at the end of the day and write down your FOOD intake. Analyze what you ate and decide what changes you need to make. It will also cause you think twice about what you put in your mouth—especially since you know you will have to write it down.

The letter "E" in L.I.F.E. stands for EXERCISE.

We each have different limits when it comes to physical exercise. While this is not a book designed to give techniques or programs for working out, we all need to focus on training that strengthens our core muscle groups and builds our cardiovascular system.

When we fail to eat correctly and exercise, we will almost always suffer spiritually in the process. Some of the greatest tools I have used have been the *Body For Life* book by Bill Phillips and *The Zone* by Dr. Barry Sears. Both of these can be researched online or purchased through any major bookstore.

I also recommend talking with your physician, a nutritionist, and a personal trainer before starting any exercise or diet program. What I am advocating is a common sense diet and lifestyle that includes adequate exercise. Thirty minutes of daily exercise will generate the energy that you will need to pursue your God-given dream. So this too is a spiritual aspect of our lives.

Make Room for What's Important

Some may argue: *"My schedule is far too busy to follow this kind of regimen!"* I would respond that in the long run you are not only saving minutes, you are adding years by obeying what God has already programmed us to do. You can't afford *not* to take the time.

Each individual makes room for what is really important to him or her. I saw this illustrated a few months ago. While driving down the main boulevard of our city something caught my attention that made me laugh out loud. It was a fellow driving a small BMW convertible with a huge, brand new, still-in-the-box, 60" television crammed in the passenger seat. Without the top down it would never have fit into the car. It barely did as it was!

Obviously, he didn't want to wait on home delivery.

I laughed because I would probably do the same thing for something I really wanted.

The question is, "How important is the dream that God has placed in your heart?" Since it's so necessary for your future, you must make room for it—and do whatever it takes to see it come to pass.

It all begins with a vital relationship with the Dream Maker. So come on, together let's R.U.N. for LIFE!

Four

ALTERED BY INJURY

Consider it pure joy, my brothers, whenever you face trials of many kinds, because you know that the testing of your faith develops perseverance. Perseverance must finish its work so that you may be mature and complete, not lacking anything.
– JAMES 1:2-4

Everybody needs a dream. Dreams are what keep us alive!

When the dream awakens in our hearts, we often start out with a bang. The starting gun goes off, adrenaline shoots through our veins, and we jump off the starting block into this spiritual race with great determination and passion. This is the way the race begins. But, as it continues, obstacles appear and setbacks occur.

Nobody goes through this journey without suffering an injury. Everybody gets tripped up now and then. It's called the race of life!

Trials will come! The question is: *"How are we going to handle the tests that head our way? How will they affect us?"*

———————▲———————

Will our dreams shrink down in fear to the intimidating taunts of the Goliath of discouragement, or the giant of cancer, depression, or failure—or will we run toward the dream-killer in the name of the Lord?

David understood that God was greater than any contender. He declared: *"The battle is the Lord's"* (1 Samuel 17:47).

DREAMS AND DISAPPOINTMENTS

Think with me for a moment. Have you ever had a conversation with a person about dreams and as they're talking you can see their eyes light up for just a moment? They tell you: *"I've always wanted to be a doctor. I even started medical school. One year of classes and my mom got sick. That's when I was needed at home! I guess it wasn't in the cards for me to finish the dream! Oh well—that's life!"* And, the eyes go dim again.

Or maybe a wife: *"I always dreamed of being married and raising a family, but then I learned that I wasn't able to have kids of my own. It was devastating!"*

Another may share: *"Our marriage started out great —but then he started drinking again! So much for living happily ever after!"*

A thirty-something might say: *"I dreamed of being married by now. Hello—God? I'm beginning to think that I will always be alone."*

Dreams have a tendency to shrink when they become mixed with disappointment. Nobody makes it through this life without some setbacks and pain. Nobody!

THE STORY INSIDE THE TREE

If you have ever seen California redwood trees you are awestruck by the majesty and the rugged strength they portray. To the human eye they appear indestructible.

The inside story is even more amazing than their outward beauty. Some of these trees have stood for over two-thousand-years, recording the history about the challenges that tried to impede their growth.

A redwood can stand for two millenniums, yet in a moment come crashing down. Mighty is the fall as the earth shakes around it, and the atmosphere changes from the billowing dust cloud.

It is at that moment you can find out the true-life story of a great redwood tree. This is when the tree can be cut open revealing the life journal that has been recorded consistently for thousands of years. Each ring in the trunk represents a year in its life. A very fine ring denotes a story of drought, where there was very little growth. A thicker ring reveals an abundance of rain when all of the elements were just right.

If you follow a blemish down the trunk you might discover where lightning pierced through the bark one year. The scars inside the tree each tell the story of trials. Regardless of the drought or the lightning strikes, the tree still grew from the inside out. It continued to race towards the sky for others to look at and say with awe: *"How could a tree survive that many years?"*

It doesn't take long for every observer to conclude it is only by the grace of God that the tree has survived!

TRAGEDY AND TRIUMPH

We all experience seasons in our lives—sometimes of wonderful growth and abundance, and at other times seasons of want and drought. Even the strongest among us face problems that threaten to hinder his or her development.

There are certain individuals we encounter and think, *"There can't possibly be anything wrong with that person. "* But if you were able to look on the inside you would find scars, tragedy, and triumph.

In this life, everyone gets injured in the race.

My wife struggled with depression for seven years. Like a redwood, each ring during that time was just a fine line, and it didn't appear there was any growth at all.

I remember exactly where I was standing when she said to me, *"I just can't live like this anymore."* I recall the pain in her eyes and the hopelessness that blanketed her.

Only God understands why certain trials occur and the length of time we are to endure them. After seven years of struggle and drought, God graciously lifted that heaviness from her and today she is experiencing a wonderful extended period of growth and vitality.

To develop in strength and beauty, it is absolutely necessary to endure dark valleys. The good news is that there is a reward for those who don't give up. In James 1:2-4, he describes that there ought to be joy in suffering, but then he gives us a glimpse into the future when he says: *"Blessed is a man who perseveres under trial, because when he has stood the test, he will receive the crown of life that God has promised to those who love Him"* (verse1:12).

We could all take some coaching tips from James concerning the problems we face.

———————▲———————

***Trials will come and there is only one way out
—we have to go <u>through</u> them.***

Whatever we face, however, we can rejoice because we are not alone! Here is what the Lord promises: *"Fear not, for I have redeemed you; I have*

*summoned you by name; you are mine. When you
pass through the waters, I will be with you; and when
you pass through the rivers, they will not sweep over
you. When you walk through the fire, you will not be
burned; the flames will not set you ablaze"* (Isaiah
43:1-2).

UNLIMITED POWER

How do you respond when the heat is on and the
pressure is mounting? I want to encourage you to start
by adopting a prayer that the apostle Paul prayed for
the church in Ephesus. Make it personal: *"I pray that
my heart will be able to understand. I pray that I will
know about the hope given by God's call. I pray that
I will see how great the things are that You have
promised to those who belong to You. I pray that I will
know how great Your power is for those who have put
their trust in You. It is the same power that raised
Christ from the dead"* (Ephesians 1:18-20 NLV).

―――――▲―――――

**Be encouraged by the fact that the unlimited
power of the Almighty is available to you today.**

- *"God will strengthen you with his own great
  power so that you will not give up when
  troubles come"* (Colossians 1:11 NCV).
- *"Let us run with perseverance the race marked
  out for us"* (Hebrews 12:1).

- *"Finally, be strong in the Lord and in his mighty power"* (Ephesians 6:10).

There are truths concerning troubles we need to come to grips with.

First, problems are a part of life.

They're not an elective, but a required course. Jesus declared, *"In this world you will have trouble. But take heart! I have overcome the world"* (John 16:33).

Second, troubles are unpredictable.

To *face* problems means "to fall into trouble unexpectedly." We seldom plan for or anticipate the troubles we will experience.

Do you think Beethoven could have guessed that he would start going deaf by the time he reached twenty-eight years of age? If he had, perhaps we would not be enjoying the masterpieces of one of the greatest composers who ever lived.

We don't plan to have a medical setback, a crisis, or even a flat tire. Since we don't expect them, this is what makes them a problem. If we knew the troubles of tomorrow, we would likely quit today. And this is why God doesn't tell us in advance.

Jesus counsels: *"Therefore do not worry about tomorrow, for tomorrow will worry about itself. Each day has enough trouble of its own"* (Matthew 6:34).

Remember to refuel daily, standing in God's strength this moment. Yesterday is gone, and don't attempt to live in the future. Now is the time—and we are to use every ounce of our energy for today.

Third, troubles come in variety packs.

It's much like shopping at Costco®, the products usually don't come in small packages, but large ones, and sometimes in a variety pack.

I've heard people say, *"Trouble seems to come to me in three's."* I'm not sure about that, but one thing I know about problems is that you will never become bored with the wide variety of them. It is rare to have the same trouble again and again.

Some injuries or trials we face will be gone in a moment. It may only take a day or a week. Other wounds may require years to heal.

Think of the life of Job. It seemed his ordeal would never end. Consider Joseph or Paul who were both confined to lengthy sentences in prison cells.

"I'M REALLY NERVOUS"

I smile when I think about the eight and nine year old boys who were in the hospital room at the same time. They were in beds next to each other.

One kid leaned over to the other and asked, *"What are you in here for?"*

The second kid said, *"I'm here to have my tonsils*

out. I'm really nervous."

The first boy replied, "You've got nothing to worry about. I had that done once. They put you to sleep and when you wake up, they give you lots of Jello and ice cream. It's a piece of cake; you'll be over it just like that."

The second young man asked, "What are you here for?" He answered, "Well, I'm in here for a circumcision."

His new friend responded, "Whooooa! I had that done when I was born and I couldn't walk for a year!"

CHANGING STRATEGIES

Seriously, some wounds take longer to heal than others. There are both minor inconveniences and major crisis. Problems arrive in all kinds of shapes and sizes, but with God's help we don't have to be imprisoned by them.

———————▲———————

When we are face to face with life-altering situations it will require us to run differently than before.

When I began running, trying to get in shape, I finally started to break through and enjoy the process without struggling for oxygen. I was feeling rather good about the progress I was making in my physical conditioning. But one day I tore a calf muscle that forced me to hobble on one leg all the way home.

It took months for that muscle to heal and I had to learn to train differently or all the progress I had made would have been wasted. So, I started riding a bike.

My torn calf muscle story is probably woefully insignificant compared to the life-altering circumstances that you are facing. In fact, it's trivial in comparison to my mother and father-in-law losing their youngest son, Jared, in a motorcycle accident. All of our lives were altered when this happened. This tragic loss still makes our hearts ache.

During the final edit of this book, I am adding yet another life-altering story.

A U.S. Navy representative knocked on the door of the house of one of our beloved staff members at First Family Church.

As the father answered the door, the news was given with regret: "I'm sorry sir, we regret to inform you that your son was killed in an automobile accident yesterday afternoon."

He was only twenty years of age!

Problems come to all of our doors. For many of us, the news falling off the lips of a doctor, spouse, or, even a stranger, can change the way we do life.

The following story is used by permission. It's the family's hope that it will encourage others to endure as they Run for Life.

TRAGIC NEWS

Dan followed in his father's footsteps by taking over the family business and building it up to a level his dad would be proud. Years before, his father had died from brain cancer.

Dan admired his dad and loved the enterprise he had established. There was only one thing that Dan cherished more than business—his family. He loved his wife Kim, and their two beautiful girls more than anything in the world. Chelsea was the oldest, attending high school, and Sabrina was right on her heels. They were the center of his universe.

Tragedy struck the family out of nowhere. Sabrina was having medical complications the doctors couldn't figure out. She was nauseated and experiencing dizzy spells at school, which eventually progressed into seizures.

Even after running a battery of tests, the doctors still couldn't discover the problem. Finally, their physician ordered an MRI of the brain and that's when the entire family's world turned upside down. Their worst fears became a reality as the doctor shared the bad news, *"We've discovered a tumor on Sabrina's brain."*

It was at this point I really got to know the family.

They had always been people of faith, but this news renewed their reliance upon God. They called on the church for prayer, and every Sunday, unless there was a medical procedure or test scheduled, the family was in attendance.

A Heart that was Changed

We prayed together about how to break the news to Sabrina.

─────▲─────

We asked God for a miracle; that He would remove the tumor.

Tears flowed as we kept encouraging one another in faith. Finally, a date was set for the surgery. Everyone concluded this would be God's method to help Sabrina lead a cancer-free life.

Every Sunday, right in the center section of the sanctuary, I would catch a glimpse of Dan listening intently and grabbing every word of promise he could from the Scriptures of the day. Each week tears would stream down his face as we concluded in prayer.

Through this tragedy, somehow God was getting more of Dan's heart. His co-workers noticed a difference in him, and his family was beginning to find great strength and confidence that the Lord is in control and Jesus is the Great Physician.

We celebrated when we received the news that Sabrina's surgery was a huge success. People in many places were praying for God's grace to be poured out on her young life. This would now be the beginning of the road to recovery. You could just see the heaviness begin to lift from the family, yet the battle was far from over.

"He's Gone!"

In the midst of celebration and renewed faith another storm was brewing. Three weeks later Kim cried out, *"How much can one family take?"*

I received the news late in the evening and I rushed to the hospital. What I learned sent chills down my spine, and tears clouded my vision as I drove to be with the family. This time it was Dan. He was found unconscious in the family swimming pool.

---▲---

The paramedics were called and they quickly transported him to a nearby hospital.

When I reached the medical center a crowd had already formed outside his room. I was rushed in to his bedside where Kim stood over Dan holding his hand. *"He's gone!"* she said.

I couldn't believe it—there are no words that can change reality—only immense grief. Once again, *"How much can one family take?"*

Answers were difficult. There was only silence.

A Verse to Cling To

Overcoming one obstacle and avoiding a tragedy in Sabrina's life was exhilarating, but facing another mountain when all energy was drained seemed impossible. The autopsy determined that Dan had passed from *"rapid electrocution,"* which gave some comfort to Kim and the girls realizing that he didn't experience any suffering.

In the blink of an eye, Dan exhaled on this earth and the next breath he was inhaling the beauty of heaven.

"How did you find the motivation to go on?" I asked Kim a year later.

She replied with a verse God had given her in the midst of this tragedy: *"Trust in the Lord with all of your heart and lean not on your own understanding; in all your ways acknowledge Him, and He will make your paths straight"* (Proverbs 3:5-6).

At the funeral, our church gave the girls a gold heart-shaped locket with their father's picture inside and it had that exact passage engraved on the outside. At the time we didn't know that the Lord had spoken this same verse into Kim's heart.

Kim and her daughters are still learning to RUN for LIFE in the midst of this life-altering experience. There's not a day that goes by they don't miss Dan. Some days are better than others, but they keep running their race.

We don't understand why things like this happen, but we must be willing to cling to the same promise: *"Trust in the Lord"* with all your heart.

Whatever trials you are experiencing today, please don't give up. God's grace is capable of carrying you through.

Fourth, problems have benefits.

As written in the Phillips translation: *"Realize that they come...to produce something in you"* (James 1:2-4)

Trials have a purpose and pain can be productive and actually add value to your life. What value? James tells us how they build endurance and perseverance.

Every athlete needs resistance in order to gain new strength. Without being stretched we will never grow. Of course, none of us like to take on more than we can handle. This is why I have emphasized the need of the Holy Spirit as your Coach. When we stay in step with Him, He will take us to heights we have never before reached and places beyond our own capacity.

Remember, it is not your ability, strength, or wisdom that will allow you to accomplish your God-given dream, it is His mighty power working through you.

PURPOSE IN PAIN

Often we view trouble as God's punishment, but the Bible states just the opposite. The Lord tells us that if we are going through trials and tribulations, we should rejoice because it shows that He loves us.

When some read this they may say, "Well, I wish God would stop loving me so much!"

The truth is, the Lord loves you too much to leave you just the way you are, so He allows some pain in your life so you can grow in faith. In the process, He will develop staying power in you—the ability to persevere. He will use this experience to build character in your life.

————▲————

We must never forget that in God's Kingdom everything has a reason.

The Lord causes all things to work together for good for those that love Him and are called to accomplish His purpose (Romans 8:28).

God's Word also tells us: *"We can rejoice, too, when we run into problems and trials, for we know that they help us develop endurance. And endurance develops strength of character, and character strengthens our confident hope of salvation."* (Romans 5:3-4 NLT).

THE POWER OF HOPE

There's a wonderful book titled *Man's Search for Meaning* by Viktor Frankl. It has been named as one of the most influential books of the 21st century, selling over nine million copies in the U.S.

Frankl said: *"There is nothing in the world, I venture to say, that would so effectively help one to survive even the worst conditions as the knowledge that there is a meaning in one's life."*

He tells how he survived four Nazi concentration camps that killed his pregnant wife, his parents, and his only brother. The entrance to one of those camps had the inscription, *"Abandon all hope ye who enter here."*

Cut off from the outside world, tagged with a number, stripped of all personal identity, beaten daily, and worked to the point of physical collapse, he was powerless to avoid further suffering. He watched helplessly as malnutrition, illness, and abuse killed hundreds of fellow inmates. Yet as a professor trained in neurology and psychiatry, he also observed something clinically remarkable: that otherwise healthy prisoners died quickly if they lost hope—and that sickly inmates clung to life if they believed their existence held a purpose.

Frankl argues that while we can't avoid suffering, we can choose how to cope and find meaning in it, and move forward with renewed purpose.

Viktor Frankl figured out what the psalmist had written thousands of years before when he said: *"Find rest, O my soul, in God alone; my hope comes from him"* (Psalm 62:5).

"IT IS WELL"

Life has a way of changing course. Even great men and women struggle to navigate the stormy waters of circumstance. One of the greatest hymns ever written

93

came out of a life-altering situation.

Chicago businessman, Horatio Spafford, and his family suffered a crisis that forever changed their lives.

On November 21, 1873, his wife and four children were crossing the Atlantic on the steamship *Ville du Havre* when it was struck by an iron sailing vessel and 226 people lost their lives—including all four of Spafford's daughters. His wife survived.

Sailing to meet her in England, when Horatio passed the location where his children had drowned, he took out a pen and wrote these words:

> *When peace, like a river, attendeth my way,*
> *When sorrows like sea billows roll;*
> *Whatever my lot, Thou hast taught me to say,*
> *It is well, it is well with my soul.*

This heartfelt hymn continues to encourage millions today. Yes: *"We have this hope as an anchor for the soul, firm and secure"* (Hebrews 6:19). The name of our Hope is Jesus.

STAY CONFIDENT

When we are facing life-altering circumstances, we can remain assured the Lord is at work in our lives. There is nothing too difficult for you and God together. Paul tells us to be *"confident of this, that He who began a good work in you will carry it on to completion until the day of Christ Jesus"* (Philippians 1:6).

Our emotions may change frequently, but God's Word remains steadfast forever. We can find evidence all around us of His faithfulness.

————▲————

Even though it seems the hardships of life may swallow you up, hang in there. God is at work!

Scripture declares: *"For everything that was written in the past was written to teach us, so that through endurance and the encouragement of the Scriptures we might have hope"* (Romans 15:4).

A PACT BETWEEN FATHER AND SON

Perhaps you have heard of Derek Redmond. It's not a name from the headlines that conjures up memories of Olympic gold medals, but the heart inside of Redmond defines the essence of human spirit.

Redmond arrived at the 1992 Olympic Summer Games in Barcelona determined to win a medal in the 400–meter race. The color of the medal was meaningless; he just wanted to win one. Just one. He had been forced to withdraw from the 400-meter race at the 1988 Games in Seoul, only ten minutes before the race, because of an Achilles tendon injury.

After undergoing five surgeries, he was ready to make another attempt at qualifying for the Olympics. He was the same runner who had shattered the British 400-meter record at the age of nineteen. So when the 1992 Games arrived, this was his time, his moment and his stage to show the world how good he really was.

Derek's father Jim had accompanied him to Barcelona, just as he did for all world competitions. They were as close as a father and son could be. When Derek ran, it was as if his dad were running right next to him. Then the day of the race arrived and father and son reminisced about what it took for Derek to get to this point. They talked about ignoring past heartbreaks, past failures, and agreed that if anything bad happened, no matter what, Derek would finish the race, period.

The stadium was packed with 65,000 fans, bracing themselves for one of sport's greatest and most exciting spectacles. (You can watch it yourself on "YouTube," I'm sure you'll find it inspirational.)

The starting gun is fired and Derek creates an immediate lead. The cameras are following him as he creates a distance between the other runners. Then his dreams come to a screeching halt as he grabs the back of his right leg in pain.

He limped to an abrupt stop, fell to his knees and began sobbing as the finish line faded along with his dreams of being an Olympic champion.

ARM IN ARM

I can't tell you who won the race that day, but millions recall the moment Derek Redmond picked himself up and began to hobble on one leg towards that finish line. He was going to hold to his end of the bargain: *"Whatever happens, we are going to finish the race."*

And his father? Well, he held his end of the bargain too. He climbed out of the stands and pushed security out of the way as he ran to his son's side. With his arm around his dad's shoulder, Derek leaned into his father's strength as they continued toward the finish.

Together, arm in arm, father and son, with 65,000 people cheering, clapping and crying, finished the race just as they vowed they would. A couple of steps from the finish line, and with the crowd in an absolute frenzy, Jim released the grip he had on his son so that Derek could cross the finish line by himself. Then they celebrated together with a victory hug on the other side of the line.

With tears in Jim's eyes he said: *"I'm the proudest father alive! I'm prouder of him than I would have been if he had won the gold medal. It took a lot of guts for him to do what he did."*

Derek may not have taken home a medal that day, but as far as millions of fans are concerned—Derek, you are more than an Olympic champion. You are an inspiration to the world to never give up!

"Well Done!"

There are millions of hurting, injured people on our planet. Your life may have been altered, either emotionally or physically, and you may have felt like giving up. But hold on!

Your Father in heaven left the stands a long time ago to come along side and help you complete the race. I can't wait to hear the sound of His voice when we all cross that finish line someday: *"Well done my good and faithful son. Well done!"*

Until then, let's KEEP RUNNING!

FIVE

ADRENALINE RUSH

"You come against me with sword,
spear, and javelin, but I come against you
in the name of the Lord Almighty."
– 1 SAMUEL 17:45

It is safe to say that the sound of one hundred thousand people cheering in the Beijing Olympic Stadium sent chills down every athlete's spine. But it produced more than a feeling of excitement; it was a massive shot of adrenaline causing athletes to compete at a higher level than they ever dreamed possible.

The "Bird's Nest" was created to host the track and field competition events as well as set the standard for what has become the greatest opening and closing ceremonies in Olympic history. The rigorous training of dream-filled champions combined with the electric environment of capacity crowds cheering with enthusiasm produced 43 world and 132 Olympic records. That's the power of an adrenaline rush!

THEY'RE CHEERING YOU ON!

Shhhhh! Can you hear the distant roar? It's the

99

sound of people cheering! Can you picture the stadium? Can you hear the champions of the ages urging you on as you run?

- Noah shouts, *"Never give up!"* One hundred and twenty years of preaching and not one single convert makes him an expert on endurance.

- Moses is yelling at the top of his lungs, *"Don't be afraid, God is with you."*

- Abraham, Isaac, and Jacob are standing up in the box seats, discussing how well you're running. *"This kid has promise!"*

- Joseph stands up and says, *"Keep dreaming! Keep running!"*

- Esther calls outs, *"This is your moment in history!"*

- David assures, *"I knew you could do it!"*

- Job is standing with a box of popcorn and an ice cream bar and shouts, *"It could be worse!"*

- Peter offers encouragement, *"You're almost home!"*

- Paul stands up and says *"Don't look back, forget the past, let it go...come on! You can make it!"*

- Thomas shouts, *"Keep believing!"*

In the stands we see the woman who was at the well with Jesus, never looking so beautiful. And there's the Philippian jailer, pumping his fist in the air, and he's calling your name.

Look a little closer and you can imagine your loved ones standing with a smile saying, *"See you when you cross the finish line."*

"I'M GOING TO HELP YOU"

Heads begin to turn as Jesus walks down from the back of the stadium. He touches the shoulder of every champion as He walks by. There is the widow Jesus spoke of who put the two mites in the offering plate. She's jumping and shouting your name, *"Keep running! Keep running!"*

She grows quiet as Jesus walks by. She has seen that look in His eye before. He is about to speak.

Jesus makes his way to center arena and puts His index finger up to his lips as He calls the crowd to draw silent, *"Shhhhhhhhh."*

He is walking your way and you are about to have a conversation with the Creator of the universe. Your heart is pounding and your eyes are fixed as He leans close and cups His nail-pierced hands around your ear. He speaks into your life like only a veteran Coach can: *"I'm going to help you win this race. Follow Me!"*

"That Was Awesome!"

It's amazing what adrenaline can do.
Peter felt it when he stepped out of the boat and onto the water.

---------▲---------

As he began to walk, his heart began to pump much faster than normal. It was racing even more when he began to sink!

Can you imagine the excitement he must have felt as Jesus reached out His hand, lifted him back out upon the water, giving him the ability to walk all the way back to the boat?

I can almost see Peter climbing back into that vessel, pausing for a moment and saying "That was awesome!"

"Give Me This Mountain!"

Moses experienced an adrenaline rush on the shores of the Red Sea.

- Esther felt it as she approached the King.

- Mary Magdalene felt it when she looked into the empty tomb.

- Joshua felt it when the walls began to shake.

- Joseph felt it when he saw his brothers.

- Shadrach, Meshach, and Abednego felt it when they refused to bow down to a golden idol.

- Daniel experienced it when he had his first dream.

- Caleb, at the age of 85 as he shouted, *"Give me this mountain!"*

- The blind man felt it when his eyes were opened by the Creator of life.

- The women caught in adultery felt it when she faced her accusers.

- Jesus, Himself, felt it in the Garden of Gethsemane.

You have experienced it too. It's called an adrenaline rush!

RAISING THE BAR

God designed our lives and our bodies to deal with moments that challenge our faith. I can't find evidence anywhere in Scripture that promotes a "Play it safe" lifestyle.

I believe in being well-balanced, but balance is not biblical without occasional heavy doses of faith-stirring experiences. It's these moments of a spiritual "rush" that mark and motivate us to reset the bar of belief and expectation. If we are never challenged or pushed it would be impossible for us to grow.

————————▲————————

Regardless of modern philosophy, advanced psychology, and wonder drugs, the laws of God still remain. We were born for adrenaline!

The Lord created us to take on tasks that seem to stretch us beyond our human capacity. These faith-challenged moments call us out of our comfort zone.

Look back over the growth rate of your spiritual journey. When did it begin to rise? When did it peak?

If you were to overlay that chart with the problems and trials that have appeared in your life, you will probably find a consistent pattern that there was substantial growth when you faced challenges.

I'm sure there were days when you wanted out of a situation, but God had you right in the middle of it for a purpose. In such times, your faith began to soar to the level of the circumstance.

Helen Keller said: *"Security is mostly a superstition. It does not exist in nature nor do children of men as a whole experience it. Life is either a daring adventure or it's nothing at all."*

So my charge to you is, let's Run for Life.

A CLOUD OF WITNESSES

One of the most noticeable characteristics of the

Roman Empire was their love for competitive sports. In every major city you would find a gigantic amphitheater designed for sporting events. Enormous structures tier upon tier upon tier, housing thirty to fifty thousand people.

When the Roman Coliseum was packed with cheering spectators, the roar was deafening. In fact, one emperor was so stunned by the noise when he walked in and the decibel level so intense, that it physically threw him backwards. The electric atmosphere of people cheering wildly motivated the athletes beyond human ability.

The writer of Hebrews is describing a heavenly coliseum. Tier upon tier is full of champions that have run this race before and are now cheering your name. In this environment, surrounded by *"such a great cloud of wittnesses,"* he is asking you to *"throw off everything that hinders...and let us run with perseverance the race"* (Hebrews 12:1).

David, Moses, and Esther are calling out your name. Why? Because they want you to finish the race. They know, first-hand, the importance of never quitting and understand what is awaiting you on the other side of the finish line.

Yes, they are pulling for you to win, but also know it's not easy on the track of life. So they encourage, *"Run! Run! And don't you dare give up! You can make it! We're waiting for you!"*

There is a common denominator connecting every Christ follower. We each have to strive, strain, stretch, and push to finish the course. Nobody gets off the hook easily. It takes endurance.

Beyond Jericho

The word *"race"* in the Greek is *"agonai,"* from which we derive our English word "agony."

It's not too encouraging to think of running in pain and agony, but let's be realistic. We will all have to push through "quitting points" if we want to succeed.

Expect every step to be contested by the enemy of your soul.

Long ago, God told Joshua to cross over the Jordan River into the Promised Land. As an inheritance, the Almighty declared: *"I will give you every place where you set your foot"* (Joshua 1:3).

Sounds easy enough, doesn't it? There were only a couple of drawbacks. The land which Joshua had set his heart on was occupied by huge armies, even giants. Plus, it was surrounded by the roughest possible terrain. But God tells him: *"Go! I've given you the land. Run your race that is set before you. It will not be easy."*

The battle of Jericho was just a stepping stone. God's people had to fight for every city, every acre of ground, every field, every hill, every mountain, and every meadow.

This is the way the Lord works through His people—in partnership. Thankfully, He empowers us with His strength along the way.

CHEERS AND JEERS

Just because you're a Christ follower doesn't mean that life is going to be easy. No, Satan can cause it to be difficult and demanding. He will oppose you every inch of the way, but you have been commanded to fix your eyes on Jesus (Hebrews 12:2) and finish the course He has set.

―――――▲―――――

Remember, all of heaven is rooting for you! Those shouts of encouragement are intended to give you a "rush," a burst of energy to keep you going one more mile.

The devil will attempt to trip you up and weigh you down. Yes, there are cheers echoing in heaven, but there are also jeers surrounding you from the enemy camp. The battle rages, with the voices from each side growing louder and louder.

The Bible states: *"You were running a good race. Who cut in on you and kept you from obeying the truth? That kind of persuasion does not come from the one who calls you"* (Galatians 5:7-8).

THE VOICE OF FEAR

Who are you listening to these days? Who changed the frequency? Where did you take a wrong turn to get off the path to which God has called you?

Perhaps you can identify the following voices of dream-crushers. It could be that you have listened to the relentless voice of FEAR.

This is the same discouraging voice which rang through the enemy lines between the Philistine army and the Israelites as fear spoke through a giant named Goliath (1 Samuel 17). He stood over nine feet tall, shaking a spear the size of a tree. His armor alone weighed 125 pounds, not counting the bronze that covered his legs.

————▲————

The harsh, loud voice of this enemy
had paralyzed the armies of Israel from
pursuing their dream. They made no progress
for forty days and forty nights.

Every morning Goliath strutted in front of the Israelite army shouting defiantly: *"Is there any man big enough, bad enough to fight me among the entire army of Israel? Is there anybody out there? Can you just pick one and send him my way?"*

Each dawn, a fresh layer of fear blanketed God's people and at each sunset a new weight of discouragement was laid upon their shoulders.

David arrives on the scene like a school boy with his brown sacked lunch. He is mesmerized and baffled by the immobility of God's entire army because of one giant.

Young David approached King Saul and said, *"Don't worry about this Philistine because I will go fight him."*

It wasn't very convincing to the king and he replied, *"Don't be ridiculous. There is no way that you can fight this Philistine and possibly win."*

But David didn't stand around listening to the petrified armies of Israel the past forty days and nights. He didn't lend his ear to the screaming giant from Gath. Instead, he had been in communion with the Lord in a field where he took care of his father's sheep.

There was a more dominate voice gaining David's attention. It was the voice of God reminding him, *"Greater is He that is in you than he that is in the world. There is nothing that can be formed against you that can prosper."*

And now that he was on the edge of the battle, he heard God say, *"This giant may be tall, but the taller he is, the harder he will fall!"*

David walked through every voice of fear that tried to block him from pursuing his dream. He walked past the ridicule of his brothers, ignored the patronizing of the king, marched through the heckling warriors of Israel, and he interrupted the slanders of Goliath.

Then, armed with only a slingshot, small stones, and a determination to silence the voice of fear, he took off running towards his dream. Whatever stood between David and his God-given objective was about to be run over—and in this case, Goliath was in for the shock of his life.

FIGHT OR FLIGHT?

The burst of exhilaration in David seemed to last

for years. He moved from one challenge to another in his spiritual race. But all along, God was speaking to him and would continuously supply power and wisdom, allowing him to run through the quitting points and finish the race.

A frequent phrase used to describe an influx of adrenaline is "fight or flight." When danger comes our way there is an instinctive behavior the Creator has placed in us that is triggered, and it relays an instant message from our brain to the rest of our body. Our blood vessels dilate, air passages expand, the heart pumps blood at higher levels and immediately we become capable of extraordinary responses. Adrenaline makes it possible to do what we could not normally do.

GRANDMA TO THE RESCUE!

My grandmother was bed-ridden by cancer when I was a little boy. She was a true saint and always looking out for the interest of others. Because of the disease, she was no longer able to help people in need; rather, she had to accept the help of others.

Grandma needed assistance sitting up, eating, and even rolling over to her side. One day while she was resting, I went outside to find something to do, and to my surprise I found a hornets nest. In all honesty, I should say the hornets found me.

While I was throwing rocks, I learned the expression, "stirring up a hornets nest."

It didn't even take a direct hit to send them into attack mode.

Seemingly, the entire hive came after me, sending me running into the house screaming at the top of my lungs. My grandmother shot up in bed, pulled the oxygen off her face, and met me at the door to save me from my stupidity, and the hornets!

————————▲————————

That's adrenaline! It is amazing what a person can do when their heart rate is stimulated.

I'm referring to more than just a natural response to fear. There is a spiritual stimulation that God gives us for those times when giants stand between us and our destiny. In such moments you will face *three* stages of adrenaline: fight, flight, or fright.

THE FRIGHT FACTOR

The whole army of Israel stood paralyzed like a deer staring into the headlights. They didn't fight or run away. Their indecision caused the third stage, fright, to kick in and this is where they remained; frozen in the land of fear for those forty days and nights.

Is there anything crippling your faith these days? The longer you listen to fear, the longer you are going to stay immobilized. The more you listen to the jeers of the dream crusher, the more he will have control over you.

Some of us have been at a spiritual standstill longer than Saul's armies. And the more you listen to the enemies voice, the more convinced you become that God can't or won't answer. Have you ever thought to yourself, *"Well, The Lord did it for them, but He won't do it for me?"*

Make no mistake. God is more than able to perform miracles far beyond your thinking. Let your faith be lifted to a brand new level.

David certainly didn't let fear or fright set in. He responded with fight. Sure, there are situations when we need to run away, just as Joseph ran away from temptation, but this was David's time to fight.

When David announced: *"You come against me with sword, spear, and javelin, but I come against you in the name of the Lord"* (1 Samuel 14:45), his bold declaration became a point of no return. It's like jumping off a cliff. Once your feet leave the rock it's too late to change your mind!

At that moment David must have felt the mighty power of God as those words left his lips. As he took the leap of faith, he shouted to Goliath: *"This day, you are going to fall!"*

The adrenaline rush was undoubtedly greater than when he confronted the bear, or the lion in the field as he watched over his father's flocks. Once again he found himself standing before an immense problem, but this time his decision would shape a nation's destiny.

This was a defining moment in David's life—and, like David, we never forsee when our defining moment may come. The next time you face a seemingly insurmountable mountain, it might very well be placed there by the Almighty so you can change the world!

David had confidence that God would supply him with the strength and wisdom needed to overcome this barrier to victory. That assurance had been built up over the years by God's perfect track record. The Lord had never failed him before, and David was certain God would be with him when he faced Goliath.

THE VOICE OF TEMPTATION

Friend, be wise and courageous against the fear that will try to control your mind. But also, be vigilant to the voice of temptation. James 1:12 promises a reward to those that resist the lures of the enemy: *"Blessed is the man who perseveres under trial, because when he has stood the test, he will receive the crown of life that God has promised to those who love him."*

As time progressed, King David mastered the art of overcoming the voice of fear, but he succumbed to the voice of temptation. It's a common flaw that has crushed the dreams of many great men and women in history. This message seems strongest when things are going well in our lives, causing us to say, *"Why change course when this has worked for so long?"*

Your adversary knows your weak spots, and when to advance his plan of attack. The apostle Paul confirmed this fact in his letter to the believers at Corinth: *"No temptation has seized you except what is common to man"* (1 Corinthians 10:13).

The most dangerous period in a believer's life is not when we are in the midst of a trial or challenge, it is when things are going well and we let down our guard. This was certainly the case for King David.

Scripture records: *"In the spring of the year, when kings normally go out to war...David stayed behind in Jerusalem"* (2 Samuel 11:1 NLT).

Late one warm afternoon, after his midday rest, King David got out of bed and looked over the city from his penthouse. He was probably yawning and stretching when Bathsheba caught his eye as she bathed in full view of the king's window. We will never know if there was indiscretion on Bathsheba's part, but it was a tremendous opportunity for Satan to stop the momentum of David's "Run for Life."

The rest is archived in history for all to read. The devastation of murder, the death of a son, the brokenness of sin, and the emptiness of selfishness became David's dark memoir.

———————▲———————

Nobody escapes unscathed when they become ensnared by the voice of temptation. It will always take you further than you want to go and cost you more than you want to pay.

The mission of the enemy of our soul has never been to show us a good time. He seeks to kill, steal, and ultimately destroy our lives and extinguish the flames of our dreams.

When we follow temptation, it will always hurt and devastate the people closest to us.

A FOOLISH PURSUIT

We have a Chocolate Labrador and a Golden Retriever as a part of our family, and these dogs seem to look for trouble.

It was about one o'clock in the morning on New Year's day, and we were winding down from the celebration of another year. We began to smell a hint of a skunk and closed the living room window. The odor grew more pungent as the skunk moved closer to the house. We opened the back door and instantly realized that both dogs had been sprayed in the face. It was awful!

Trying to think quickly, I opened my son's sliding door that leads to the shower next to his room. My plan was to lead the dogs to the shower and clean them up. However, the dogs began to roll around on the carpet trying to rub off the skunk oil.

The whole house smelled for days because of the lure of temptation. Our dogs thought they could attack a skunk! This foolish pursuit ended up adversely affecting our whole family.

––––––––**A**––––––––

We must be alert and stay away from
the beguiling lure of temptation—for your
sake and the ones you love.

The Voice of Shame

Another enemy that will compete for your attention is the sabotaging voice of shame. It is persuasive and adds a spirit of heaviness that drags down your spiritual pace.

We all have things we don't like about ourselves, but we must always remember that we are a work in progress!

When shame starts to speak to you, remember how far you have come rather than how far you need to go.

A few years ago we rescued a lost dog and brought him home to take care of until we could return him to his rightful owners. We were sure that posters would go up around the neighborhood describing this beautiful Chocolate Lab puppy. In actuality, weeks went by without any clue as to the owner. It took only a few nights to understand why this puppy had been abandoned.

He howled all night long and we were now the proud owners of the "night howler!" We gave him the name "Chip" and welcomed him into the family.

Over several months we started seeing signs that this dog had been abused; no doubt because of his chronic howling. I'm no dog whisperer but it was fairly obvious that this had a negative effect on Chip's personality.

He was territorial and aggressive with other dogs, and, more seriously, with people. One friend nick-named him, "Crazy Eyes", because of his erratic behavior. Visitors would go to pet him and he would snap into attack mode. (By the way, I know a few people like this too!)

Our neighbors were concerned when they would see Chip because of his hostility. We finally decided to hire a dog trainer to keep peace in the neighborhood. We worked with Chip for months and saw tremendous improvement. However, it didn't matter how much progress the dog made, he still had his old reputation in the neighborhood.

Today, countless people have come through our doors and can tell you he is a playful and obedient part of the family. Others may remind us of what he *used* to be, but we are encouraged by how far Chip has come along. We believe in him and we see signs that the best is still ahead.

God views you in light of your potential. Remember, He is creating a masterpiece and the unveiling will ultimately take place. The Lord doesn't dwell on your past failures and overwhelm you with guilt. When God speaks into your life He will always lead you closer to Himself.

So when the degrading voice of shame is trying to hijack your attention, remind yourself how far you have come and that it only gets better from here on out. Choose to fill your mind with the awesome promises of God.

THE VOICE OF PRIDE

There is another danger. The same enemy of your dreams that will paralyze you with fear, trip you up with temptation, or sabotage you with shame, can also puff you up with pride.

British author John Ruskin observed: *"There is no smaller package in the world than someone who is all wrapped up in himself."*

Pride is an attitude which declares: *"I don't need God. I can handle this on my own."*

Before we dismiss the notion that we don't tune into the voice of puffed up pride, let me ask you a few questions. How is your daily time with God going? A prayerless life is a prideful life. It is subtle arrogance to think that we can handle the day before us in our own strength. This is why Solomon's book of wisdom warns us: *"Pride goes before destruction, a haughty spirit before a fall"* (Proverbs 16:18).

Permit me another question: How generous have you been lately with your time, money, and talents? A stingy life is also prideful because it carries the notion: *"I have earned everything I have and it is solely mine to enjoy."*

Scores of sections of Scripture teach us that we are blessed to be a blessing. A dream-pursuing life is not one of accumulation, but rather of distribution.

One final question and I'll stop probing: How much credit do you take for the good things that happen to you?

————▲————

When we start to think that we have arrived because of our superior intelligence and uncanny way with life management, we have been duped by the seduction of pride.

If we look closely into our inner man or woman, I believe we will find evidence of the shallow voice of pride speaking to each of us. It is most effective at low volumes rather than the mental images of a Mohammad Ali pumping his fist in the air proclaiming: *"I am the greatest!"* Normally, we just start to think a little too highly of ourselves.

THE RIGHT FREQUENCY

If we are going to be successful, we must learn how to tune out the negative voices vying for our attention and adjust to the heavenly frequencies. Like the radio, you can choose the station that you are going to listen to.

Some people say, *"All I ever have are negative thoughts!"* This is because you have only dialed the negative channels of life.

Our church dealt with frequency issues every week with our wireless microphones. We finally became frustrated because the frequencies would randomly cancel each other out during the services. We asked an expert for advice, and he brought a piece of equipment to the church that identified the frequencies occupying the airwaves in the auditorium. He then readjusted the wireless microphones to an unoccupied channel so that they wouldn't have to compete for the same signal.

The same is true in our lives. Some of you may be trying to fight each of these different voices, when all along you just need to tune into a whole new channel. God still speaks today, but we have to be tuned in to Him.

Jesus said: *"My sheep listen to my voice; I know them, and they follow me"* (John 10:27).

Here are the top three ways that God communicates with us:

1. He speaks through His written Word.

This is God's primary way of speaking into our lives. God's word is alive—much more than pages bound in leather. When you take time daily to read the Bible, you are giving God an opportunity to speak into your soul.

2. He speaks through impressions.

My life has been defined by the small impressions the Lord has given to me through an idea, an act of kindness, a difficult conversation, wisdom in the moment of need, or a note of encouragement to a friend. For example, this book began as a simple idea God laid upon my heart to inspire others.

Remember, however, impressions from the Lord never contradict His written Word.

3. He speaks through the counsel of other people.

To test the validity of what I believe the Lord is saying to me, I share it with a respected, trusted friend. Why? Because: *"As iron sharpens iron, so one man sharpens another"* (Proverbs 27:17).

On occasion, I will seek advice and other times

God just seems to put individuals in my path to elevate me with an encouraging word. I would still be spinning my wheels in some instances if it were not for God's gift of the counsel with which He has blessed me.

However, the most valuable relationships I have are not the ones who always agree with me (although I really appreciate this). Rather, it is with individuals who gently guide me in the right direction by reminding me of my potential. Often this may require a tough conversation, or perhaps a refreshing word. That's when I look to heaven and respond to the Lord with gratitude for sending someone to lift me up.

FEEL THE RUSH!

Dozens of voices are vying for your attention —including those of fear, temptation, shame, and pride. Will you listen to the enemy of your soul or your Savior? Will you fall along the way or keep persevering until you achieve the crown of life?

Friend, you are in an eternal race, and I can tell you who wants you to win.

Can you hear the roar echoing from the heavenly stadium? They are calling out your name!

Feel the RUSH, run the race!

Six

FINISH EMPTY

For I am already being poured out like a drink offering, and the time has come for my departure. I have fought the good fight, I have finished the race, I have kept the faith. Now there is in store for me the crown of righteousness, which the Lord, the righteous Judge, will award to me on that day—and not only to me, but also to all who have longed for his appearing.

– 2 TIMOTHY 4:6-8

I have met plenty of *"Ideas"* type people in my lifetime. These are innovators who are always thinking about a "new idea" that could revolutionize the modern world. The only problem is, most of them have never executed a plan to actually realize a creative concept. The idea remains in the "To Do" file located somewhere in the back in their mind. Their mantra appears to be: *"Someday I'll get to that. And when I do, it'll be amazing!"*

In the meantime, they keep creating new ideas to talk about, but unfortunately, these also go into the bulging file of other undeveloped plans.

These same individuals become frustrated when someone else comes along and successfully produces a similar product. Indignant, they protest, *"They stole my idea!"* No, they didn't. They executed a plan to see a vision move to completion. They finished what they started. The difference between a dreamer and one who is living the dream is *execution.*

Every April 15th I say the same thing; *"Next year, I'm going to complete my taxes early."* But when next year comes around I find myself filing another extension.

It would be much better if I would just take care of the matter so it doesn't weigh on my mind. Procrastination always has a tendency to deplete our energy levels. If it is important, we should finish the task and move on to the next challenge.

The truth is, it feels great when the job is done in a timely manner. The completion of a dreaded term paper, a well crafted song, or a college degree deserves a victory lap. An improved scorecard for a golfer brings motivation to keep improving. The satisfaction of reaching a goal builds confidence to do it again.

On the other hand, there are some who take on a quitter's mentality. This defeatist attitude begins to harden like concrete with every project that remains undone. The more we give up in the middle of an undertaking, a race, or a relationship, the greater the possibility we are going to take on such a mentality.

BREAK THE CYCLE

Many buy into the lie that says: *"I'm not as gifted as other people. If I had more talent I would make it to the end."*

Drifting into this mindset will cause you to resent winning altogether. We need to break the cycle. Instead, it's time to start building up our confidence level by winning a few of life's races. You may need to say: *"I'm going to stick with this job for a year, even if it kills me!"* Or, perhaps you need to make the commitment: *"I'm going to go to church every weekend for a month. I'm not going to miss a week!"*

If clutter is a problem in your life, maybe you just need to clean one room and have a victory party. Celebrate the triumph!

If exercise is a problem, begin by taking a walk for just half an hour at the end of your day.

Read a book this month! Even a small one will give you a sense of satisfaction for completing a task. Not to mention, you might enjoy the book.

———————▲———————

Do something from start to finish and take a moment to congratulate your accomplishment.

This is what it takes to begin forming the habits of a winner.

Finish the Task

What is the one thing in your life right now that is really nagging you (besides your spouse)! Name a project that is still incomplete. What is keeping you from personal growth?

It could be working toward a license or a certification so you can excel in your job. It might be starting a ministry that God keeps prodding you to begin. Whatever it is, realize that your heavenly Father is glorified when we finish the tasks that are before us. As Paul says: *"Whatever you do, do it all for the glory of God"* (1 Corinthians 10:31).

Develop a winner's attitude!

If God begins a work in your life, I can assure you that He will give you the determination and resources to reach the goal.

————▲————

All you need is the right combination of faith and works. In other words, make sure your expectations are rising and your feet are moving!

The Lord will make sure you achieve the objective.

We not only serve a God who is faithful, but One who finishes what He starts. He will complete what He has begun in us because He is *"the author and finisher of our faith"* (Hebrews 12:2 NKJV).

What Happened to the Dream?

When we visit our family in Ohio, I always look for one particular house along a winding country road. The home stands out because the builder started the renovations on an existing property with a clear dream in his mind—as if he were making a statement to the neighborhood. It was no longer going to be the smallest house on the block. Rather, the owner was taking one giant step forward to create the mansion he envisioned. It was as if he were saying, *"There's a new kid on the block."*

This country house was turning into a beautiful residence before everyone's eyes.

It was obvious the house was going to be a spectacular showhouse. There were pallets of high quality decorative rock that would soon be attached to the face of the structure. You could see the beauty of the elegant chandeliers hanging from the great cathedral ceiling in full view from the picture window.

It started out with a flurry of renovations, but as time marched on, the project began to stall. Each year we went back to visit, I was amazed at how little had been accomplished. It became evident that something was desperately wrong. Weeds were growing profusely around the shell of an unfinished dream. Apparently, the builder did not do a cost analysis when he started the project.

Calculate the Cost

Think about the words of Jesus: *"Don't begin until*

you count the cost. For who would begin construction of a building without first calculating the cost to see if there is enough money to finish it? Otherwise, you might complete only the foundation before running out of money, and then everyone would laugh at you" (Luke 14:28-29).

Why would God's Son talk about building—and the price involved? Because He had just finished explaining that if you are planning to enter this spiritual race of following Him, you must understand that there is a cost of admission. What is the price? *Everything!*

Before you close this book and walk away disappointed, you need to know that in God's economy, you will gain far more than you ever invest.

Many start their spiritual race, but somewhere along the way they stop running. Some give up because they can't handle the heat of criticism from friends. Others stop to chase after the riches of the world. Still others bail out because they get sidetracked or discouraged by the problems of life. Then there are those who walk away because a church member offended them.

But others finish the race—and, thank God, these special few will know the thrill of victory and enjoy the everlasting benefits of endurance.

LEARN TO RUN

To help you complete the spiritual course God has placed you on, let me share these principles:

First, learn to run with no regrets.

At the end of Paul's mission, with victory in sight, there were no statements of "what might have been." Instead, he wrote to young Timothy: "*I have fought the good fight. I have finished the race. I have kept the faith*" (2 Timothy 4:7).

------------▲------------

Without excuses, he was ready to receive the "crown of righteousness" awaiting him at the finish line.

At the time of this writing, Paul is looking older than his age. His body is crippled from the many beatings for his testimony of Christ. The scars on his body are evidence of the serious blows from floggings, being stoned (rocks, not drugs), and being shipwrecked. He is sitting in a dark, dank Roman prison cell, the equivalent of death row, awaiting execution as his failing eyesight catches a single ray of light streaming through the prison bars. The light and an impression from God inspires him to grab parchment and pen as he drafts one final letter of instruction to his son in the faith, Timothy.

He begins this second letter with the words: *"Timothy, my dear son."* We can feel the warmth and imagine the fire in his eyes. "*Grace, mercy, and peace from God the father and Christ Jesus, our Lord. I thank God.*" Thank God? He is chained, beaten, deeply bruised and scarred and he is thankful? *"I thank God whom I serve as my forefathers did with a clear conscience"* (2 Timothy 1:2-3). Then he added: *"I have no regrets"* (verse 11 TM).

His body may be feeble but his eyes are ablaze, his heart is beating strong and fast. As he puts the pen down he quickly forms the letter into a perfect scroll and passes it through the prison bars like a baton. His close friend Dr. Luke carefully takes the message and it won't be long before Timothy will break the seal and publicly read the final words from his mentor and hero.

———————▲———————

Timothy must have been filled with excitement when the message started pouring off the page and into his heart.

Paul refused to look back on his past mistakes, nor did he focus on the first three quarters of his life when he was self-absorbed. He chose to throw off the sins that had tried to weigh him down. We can imagine him saying: *"Yesterday Ended Last Night!"*

Once he was consumed with degrees, advancements, and pride. He remembered the day on the road to Damascus when Christ interrupted his journey—and he started pouring his life out for others. He was now guided by a new set of values. He finally understood what really mattered.

WHAT REALLY MATTERS?

It's a tragedy to waste our precious days on things

that will crumble to dust.

I've been a chronic asthmatic since I was a small boy and have experienced my fair share of close calls. I won't bore you with details, but there was one major incident where I was reminded what is truly important.

When you come close to drawing your last breath, you think more clearly than ever before. In such moments you understand what is important and what is not.

At one particular low point, I remember these words flooding through my mind: *"When all is said and done, there's only one thing that really matters: RELATIONSHIP—with God and with other people."*

This is what lasts forever.

As we come close to the autumn of our lives, we don't think about spending more time at the office or adding another thousand dollars to our nest egg. No, we gather our family as close as possible so we can enjoy our final moments in relationship.

THE CITY OF REGRET

Author Larry Harp wrote a story titled *"The City of Regret."* It is definitely food for thought:

> *I had not really planned on taking a trip this time of year, and yet I found myself packing rather hurriedly. This trip was going to be unpleasant and I knew in advance that no real good would come of it. I'm talking about my annual "Guilt Trip."*

I got tickets to fly there on Wish I Had airlines. It was an extremely short flight. I got my baggage, which I could not check. I chose to carry it myself all the way. It was weighted down with a thousand memories of what might have been. No one greeted me as I entered the terminal to the Regret City International Airport. I say international because people from all over the world come to this dismal town.

As I checked into the Last Resort Hotel, I noticed that they would be hosting the year's most important event, the Annual Pity Party. I wasn't going to miss that great social occasion. Many of the towns leading citizens would be there.

First, there would be the Done family, you know, Should Have, Would Have and Could Have. Then came the I Had family. You probably know ol' Wish and his clan. Of course, the Opportunities would be present, Missed and Lost. The biggest family would be the Yesterday's. There are far too many of them to count, but each one would have a very sad story to share.

Well, to make a long story short, I went to this depressing party knowing that there would be no real benefit in doing so. And, as usual, I became very depressed. But as I thought about all of the stories of failures brought back from the past, it occurred to me that all of this trip and subsequent "pity party" could be canceled by ME! I started to truly realize that I did not have to be there. I didn't have to be depressed. One thing kept going through my mind, I CAN'T CHANGE YESTERDAY, BUT I DO HAVE THE POWER TO MAKE TODAY A WONDER-FUL DAY.

I can be happy, joyous, fulfilled, encouraged, as well as encouraging. Knowing this, I left the City of Regret immediately and left no forwarding address. Am I sorry for mistakes I've made in the past? YES! But there is no physical way to undo them.

So, if you're planning a trip back to the City of Regret, please cancel all your reservations now. Instead, take a trip to a place called, Starting Again. I liked it so much that I have now taken up permanent residence there. My neighbors, the I Forgive Myselfs and the New Starts are so very helpful. By the way, you don't have to carry around heavy baggage, because the load is lifted from your shoulders upon arrival. God bless you in finding this great town. If you can find it—it's in your own heart—please look me up. I live on I Can Do It Street.

Yesterday ended last night and today holds a fresh opportunity. Learn to run with no regrets.

Second, learn to run with integrity.

God is Truth and everything He creates has integrity.

Standing in line at the grocery store, I have never worried about getting home and wondering what I would find inside the yellow peel of a banana—or if a cantaloupe would contain strawberries! Why? Because when God creates something, the inside is always consistent with the outside.

One the contrary, I have met individuals who profess to be Christ followers but the way they live their lives is inconsistent with that claim. But eventually the truth is revealed. As the saying goes: *"You can fool some of the people some of the time, but you can't fool all the people all of the time."*

And we can never deceive God.

————▲————

When we lack integrity, anxiety and guilt will erode our joy and the weight of heaviness will impede the pursuit of healthy relationships and the vision the Lord has placed within us.

Here are three practices that will help develop strength from the inside out: (1) Tell the truth, (2) Keep your word, and (3) Practice what you say.

Relationships are founded on trust, and trust is built on truth—which comes from a pure heart. David said it this way: *"Surely you desire truth in the inner parts"* (Psalm 51:6).

Is it easy to live with integrity? No! It will cost us, and this is why we need God's help. The psalmist asked the Lord: *"I will be careful to live a blameless life—when will you come to help me? I will lead a life*

133

of integrity in my own home" (Psalm 101:2 NLT).

Third: Learn to run with a generous heart.

Selfishness has never made a hero of anyone. And clinging to material possessions is no way to be remembered.

Culture teaches we ought to spend our lives accumulating things, setting ourselves up for a cooling down period before we take our final breath and vanish from this earth. We are taught to work toward comfort, to make sure we have everything we need, and to protect it—*"Don't let anybody in and don't share, because you may not have enough."*

God's principles are just the opposite. We learn from the Word that real life comes as we are giving our lives away.

DAVID'S TRUE PASSION

The Old Testament paints a picture of David as a young man tending a few sheep, being a gifted musician, and a trustworthy son. But there's more to him than meets the eye. In the process of being chosen as a future king, God said about David: *"Man looks at the outward appearance, but the Lord looks at the heart"* (1 Samuel 16:7).

When the starting gun went off in David's life, he understood that he was running a race with a price tag attached. In his middle years he said: *"I will not sacrifice to the Lord my God burnt offerings that cost me nothing"* (2 Samuel 24:24).

Keep reading and you will find David approaching life's finish line. He is stretching towards the tape and generosity is flooding from his soul as though a dam had been broken loose.

This was an all-out run and David was determined not to hold one ounce back. Every last drop was going to be spent at the end.

What was his passion? It was to begin building a magnificent Temple for God.

HE GAVE EVERYTHING!

Unfortunately, David was not permitted to personally construct his dream because he had shed too much blood in battle and God was displeased (1 Kings 5:3). He was disqualified, yet he didn't give up.

Instead, David became the chief fundraiser for his son Solomon to fulfill that dream. In fact, he laid out every detail of the construction of the Temple for Solomon to follow (1 Chronicles 28).

David's heart was as young as ever, but his body had aged. After a forty-year run as King of Israel, he now called his son forward in the midst of a great national assembly.

As he walked out of the corridor with young Solomon, everyone was chanting. They knew what was about to happen: Solomon was to be declared King of Israel. David put his hand up and the crowd grew silent as he began to speak.

He looked at Solomon and said: *"My son, learn to*

know the God of your ancestors intimately. Worship and serve him with your whole heart and a willing mind. For the Lord sees every heart and knows every plan and thought. If you seek him, you will find him. But if you forsake him, he will reject you forever. So take this seriously. The Lord has chosen you to build a Temple as his sanctuary. Be strong, and do the work" (1 Chronicles 28:9-10 NLT).

After the official installation of Solomon as king, David unveiled all of the plans the Lord had given him. The master plan was no longer a hidden dream. Every detail was meticulously written out and explained—including the gold and silver to be used to make articles to serve the Lord Most High. It would be spectacular!

After directing Solomon to do the work, to never become discouraged, and to finish the task, it was now time for David's final act, the curtain was ready to come down.

Here are his powerful words: *"And now, because of my devotion to the temple of my God, I am giving all of my own private treasures of gold and silver to help in the construction"* (1 Chronicles 29:3 NLT).

He had been accumulating wealth his entire reign as king, and now it was time to give it all away for a cause greater than himself.

Then David turned to the nation of Israel and asked: *"Now then, who will follow my example and give offerings to the Lord today?"* (verse 5).

All over the place hands went up. They exclaimed: *"I will follow a dream like that."*

As David crossed the finish line of his race, not a drop was left in reserve. He finished empty.

————————▲————————

We are all too aware that the American dream is to finish full, but this is not God's plan.

Run with generosity—and give the Lord *everything!*

Fourth: Learn to run with a heart for people living far from God.

There is nothing that pleases the Father more than to see His children reaching out to people. Jesus said: *"The Son of Man came to seek and to save that which was lost"* (Luke 19:10).

The Lord is restless over those who do not know His Son. Jesus tells the story in Luke 15 of a lost sheep, a lost coin, and a lost son.

Bill Hybels has captured the heart of what Jesus was communicating to His listeners that day. In each of the three stories there were common themes:

- First, someone lost something of incredible value.

- Second, the value was so high that it demanded an all-out search to recover that which was lost.

- Third, there was enormous celebration when that which was lost was found.

It's as though Jesus were saying: *"There! Three stories back to back to back. Never underestimate the love God has for people that are wayward!"*

HE POURED HIMSELF OUT

At the end of His earthly life, Jesus was ready to break the tape of redemption's finishing line. The mission was almost fulfilled when He joined with His disciples at the Last Supper. He took a wine-filled cup in His hand and proclaimed: *"This is my blood of the covenant, which is poured out for many for the forgiveness of sins"* (Matthew 26:28).

A new world record was about to be broken, never to be surpassed. Jesus would soon accomplish the impossible, eternal life for sinners who were hopelessly lost.

The record book will stand the test of time. Jesus finished the race that was set before Him. Every step of the way He was pouring His life out for humanity. In His final moments on the cross, He would wring every last drop of love and forgiveness from His broken body:

- He poured himself out to Roman soldiers who beat Him and crowds that mocked Him: *"Father forgive them, for they do not know what they are doing"* (Luke 23:34).

- He poured Himself out to Mary and to John: *"When Jesus then saw His mother, and the disciple whom He loved standing nearby, He said to His mother, 'Woman, behold, your son!' Then He said to the disciple, 'Behold, your mother!' From that hour the disciple took her into his own household"* (John 19-26-27 NASB).

- He poured Himself out upon two thieves who were at eye level with Him. To one He said: *"Today, you will be with me in paradise"* (Luke 23:43).

The Lord came to His last breath and declared, *"It is finished!"* Everything had been given for you and for me. Jesus finished empty.

But wait! There is more. After three days, Jesus rose again! In His visit with the disciples He gave a mission for them to fulfill—and a command every believer is to follow: *"Run into all the world and proclaim the Good News of Jesus Christ! Tell the story of My saving grace. You are the light of the world. You are the salt of the earth. Show the world the way to My Father."*

Then He promised: *"I am going to empower you and be with you always! Keep telling My story and how it has changed your life. Don't keep this great treasure to yourself. Pour it out to a thirsty world. Finish empty"*

A New Start

Earlier in this chapter I told you about an

unfinished house in Ohio. Ultimately, a new owner purchased the property and completed the project. It is stunning!

Eventually, we all need to come to the realization that on our own we don't have what it takes to finish the dream the Lord started in our hearts. Somewhere we must acknowledge that we need God's help to complete what He began.

―――――▲―――――

We all search for purpose, meaning, and a reason for living. But no matter what steps we take to fill the void, there is still a spiritual vacuum.

Relationships, possessions, success, and even religion fall short of occupying this space. There is only one way to have the absolute hope of eternity in the presence of God. Our lives will always be incomplete without a growing relationship with Christ.

The greatest regret of all time is coming to the end of your life and crossing that finish line without Jesus. Facing an eternity without Christ is a foolish way to complete your race.

Perhaps God is knocking at the door of your heart right now. If you will invite Him in, He promises to give you a brand new start. Perhaps you have been running from the Lord. Please know that He never gives up His pursuit of you.

He might even use this simple book to remind you how much you matter to Him. Whatever the case, please, surrender your life to the Lord and realize the dream of a clean heart before Him!

WIN THE RACE

It is imperative that we understand the importance of Christ's death on the cross. He fulfilled the requirements of the law on behalf of mankind, to gain each person access to heaven. Without His sacrifice, there is no admission to the eternal city. Through our own efforts it is impossible to fulfill the requirements. Salvation is found through faith in Christ alone.

Some may hold the opinion that being a good person deserves access to heaven, but the Bible is quite clear that there is not one righteous person living on this planet. Not one! This means we are all in need of a Savior. Your new life in Christ can begin today as you turn to God and surrender your life to Him. You can start by softly praying these words:

Heavenly Father, I know I have sinned against You and that my sins separate me from You. I am truly sorry. I now want to turn away from my past sinful life and turn to You for forgiveness. Please forgive me, and help me avoid sinning again. I believe that your Son, Jesus Christ, died for my sins, was resurrected from the dead, is alive, and hears my prayer. I invite Jesus to become the Lord of my life, to rule and reign in my heart from this day forward. Please send your Holy Spirit to help me follow You for the rest of my life. In Jesus' name I pray. Amen.

If you just said that prayer, congratulations! Welcome to the beginning of a new life. There is a celebration going on in heaven over your decision. Your old life has passed away and you have a new identity in Christ.

————▲————

You have been forgiven for your old patterns of living, now you must follow Him in new paths of righteousness.

The first thing you should do, is tell someone about your decision to follow Christ. You will need encouragement from people that have mature Christian faith, and can help point you in the right direction.

Second, keep talking to God through prayer. At first it may seem awkward, but over time you will grow in your ability to converse with the Lord.

Third, read the Bible. Its words are your fuel for life. They will guide you into a strong relationship with God and others.

Fourth, find a solid, Bible-based Christian church to attend and continue to grow in your faith.

Finally, FINISH EMPTY! R.U.N. for LIFE!

ACKNOWLEDGMENTS

This book would not be written if not for the people in my life who dared to dream unselfishly. I am thankful to God that He saw fit to send so many wonderful individuals to share life with. This project will continually hold significant value because of the fingerprints of the many who have cheered me on through encouragement, resources, and lasting friendship.

Thanks to First Family Church and our leadership team for living these messages before they ever went to print. Special recognition goes out to Pete and Elaine Davis for their encouragement and sacrifice to make this project possible, you're the greatest!

Special thanks goes out to my family for their contribution that goes beyond a book. To my wife Tracy who dares to dream with me, you light up my life. To Matt, thanks for transcribing all of these sermons and allowing me to be inspired by God's dream in you. To Nathan, thanks for using your gifts in designing the book cover—it's exceptional, which is simply a reflection of your character. My deepest love goes out to each of you!

I'm indebted to Pastor Tommy and Luke Barnett for believing in me and inspiring me to pursue God's dream for my life. Your friendship means more than you will ever know. You have a stake in every good thing that comes out of our ministry. Thanks for dreaming with us.

Most important—Thank you Lord for loving and filling me with a worthwhile pursuit!

For Additional R.U.N For LIFE, Resources or to Schedule the Author for Speaking Engagements, Contact:

Dave Ansell
First Family Church
8434 Greenleaf Avenue
Whittier, CA 90602

Phone: 562-698-6737
Internet: www.firstfamilychurch.net